52 Florida Golf Getaways

Edward Schmidt Jr.

Pineapple Press, Inc.
Sarasota, Florida

Inquiries should be addressed to:

Pineapple Press, Inc.
P.O. Box 3889
Sarasota, Florida 34230

www.pineapplepress.com

Library of Congress Cataloging-in-Publication Data

Schmidt, Edward
        52 great Florida golf getaways / Edward Schmidt Jr.— 1st ed.
        p. cm.
        Includes index.
        ISBN 1-56164-260-6 (pbk. : alk. paper)
        1. Golf resorts—Florida—Guidebooks. 2. Golf resorts—Florida—Directories. 3. Country clubs—Florida—Guidebooks. 4. Country clubs—Florida—Directories. I. Title: Fifty-two great Florida golf getaways. II. Title.

GV982.F5 S33 2002
796.352'06'8759—dc21

                                                                2001058006

First Edition
10 9 8 7 6 5 4 3 2 1

Design by Ramonda Talkie
Printed in the United States of America

To Diane,
Paul, and Elizabeth,
who teach me
something every day
about life, love,
and golf

Acknowledgments

I WOULD LIKE to honor my father, Ed, who died while I was writing this book. More than thirty-five years ago, he introduced golf to my three brothers—Rich, Carl, and Paul—and me at a tiny, lighted par-three course in Panama City Beach. A big hug and thanks are also extended to my mother, Emily, who has been my most ardent supporter from the time I started writing seriously as a teenager.

Now, at the risk of sounding like some actor who drones on incessantly on Oscar night, I'd like to thank some people who helped me compile information and provided inspiration for this book. Among the many public relations professionals who have always given me prompt, accurate information on Florida's golf resorts and whom I consider valued friends are Krista Boling, Terry Brinkoetter, Lisa Caruso, Peggy Beucher Clark, Cindy Cockburn, Sandy Cotter, Cindy Dobyns, Kelli Kerrigan-Eshleman, Dove Jones, Al Martinez-Fonts Jr., Stephanie Klinck, Charlotte Luer, Jackie Mackay, David Matheson, Kelly Grass Prieto, Chuck Smith, Cheryl Stephenson, and Carrie Englert Zimmerman. This book was also enhanced by the insight of two of the finest people I know in the golf industry: golf course photographer Mike Klemme and golf course architect Ron Garl. Several of my long-time editor friends who helped expand my golf knowledge were also invaluable—a special thanks to Brian Adair, Pat Baldwin, Jim Bartlett, Steve Ellis, Karen Gines, Terri Hardin, Dave McCann, Larry Olmsted, and Barbara Scofidio.

Finally, I'd like to thank my golf-playing friends who have alternately made me look Tiger-like or absolutely pathetic on the golf course. A pat on the back for Glenn Alldredge, Bill Altice, Ed Beshara, Ed Beshara Jr., Roger Brasel, Bucky Fox, Bryan Heliker, Chuck Holt, Dan Koeneman, Dick Lohmann, Chuck Murray, Dave Murray, Elizabeth Schmidt, Paul Schmidt, and Lewis Wantland.

Contents

6 Southeast   125

7 Southwest   157

Category Listings   180

Category Listings (Cont'd)

Introduction

FLORIDA HAS 1,261 golf courses. Do the math: that's something like 22,698 golf holes. For a golfer, arriving in Florida is much like standing at the brink of a mammoth smorgasbord. It's loaded with so many mouthwatering golf possibilities that you almost do an about-face because you're so overwhelmed you don't know where, when, or how to begin.

I wrote this book to help you navigate Florida's wondrous buffet of fairways and greens. As an Orlando-based golf/travel writer for more than twenty years, I've traveled extensively in the state, playing courses from the Panhandle to the Keys. I've played the good, the bad, and the ugly. Speaking of the latter, I once played a course in Clearwater with greens that looked like they had been carpet-bombed. I played another in Panama City that was built on a landfill where I spotted a tire and a bottle that had somehow surfaced on the fairway.

Rest assured, though, this book is not about those courses. It's about the best courses and the best places in Florida to fulfill your dreams for a fantastic golf getaway. I'll take you to sleepy hamlets like Brooksville, where Tom Fazio has created two magnificent courses on rolling, rural terrain. I'll take you to cozy, family-owned resorts in Naples and Howey-in-the-Hills. And I'll take you to world-renowned mega-resorts like Doral, Sawgrass, and Saddlebrook. I'll also introduce you to the World Golf Village, where Hall of Fame golfers are enshrined, and the PGA Village, where the PGA of America offers three world-class courses at bargain-basement rates.

I strongly believe you can't write a good golf/travel book unless you play the game. You just miss too much. I'm an avid mid-handicapper who never saw a fairway he didn't like, unless, of course, you count that one with the Coke bottle protruding through the turf. I'm also a dedicated family man with a wife and two young children. On several occasions during the research for this book, they accompanied me to resorts and golf destinations. My wife doesn't play golf, and, as most married golfers know, leaving your non-golfing spouse in your hotel room so she can push buttons on a remote for five hours while you roam the links is a recipe for a horrendous golf vacation. For that reason, I have paid special attention to the needs and desires of non-golfers. Wherever possible, I have also highlighted activities for children as well. So, while the golfers in the family are hyperventilating about playing the newest Fazio or Nicklaus design in Florida, everyone else can enjoy nearby shopping, attractions, and recreational activities.

If Florida is a stop on your upcoming golf itinerary or you simply dream of teeing up anywhere in the state, this book will tell what to expect. With so many different golf options in Florida, I guarantee you'll find the perfect fit regardless of whether you're a struggling beginner who chops at the ball like a lumberjack or a smooth-swinging low-handicapper. And if you have one of those days when every bunker and lagoon seems to gobble up your ball and you need a calculator to count your score, rest assured that in Florida there is always an ocean, theme park, or nature preserve to renew your spirit.

Keep it in the short grass.

How to Use This Book

MANY GOLFERS mistakenly view Florida as a homogeneous chunk of land peppered with flat-as-a-pancake, palm-dotted, lagoon-laden courses. This is an unfortunate stereotype. Different regions of the state have distinct differences in climate, topography, and lifestyle. Therefore, this book is divided into seven geographic areas.

Since all golfers have specific needs, desires, and whims, I have comprehensively addressed the "personality" of each resort, destination, and attraction mentioned here. I have reviewed major golf resorts, hotels that feature play on exceptional off-site layouts, major golf-oriented attractions, and golf-happy towns and counties where the sport is king. Each review takes you on a tour, with special emphasis on the courses, accommodations, recreation activities, dining, and entertainment. Following each review is a Things to Know section, which addresses the needs of the golfer, non-golfer, and business traveler. Information includes address, phone number, website, courses, number of holes, and course designer as well as major amenities and nearby attractions such as theme parks, museums, and shopping areas. Since Florida's resorts are recognized as some of the nation's best meeting and convention venues, meeting planners will appreciate information on state-of-the-art meeting facilities offered at each site.

To avoid confusion, all references to golf course yardages are from the championship tees unless otherwise noted. You won't find any room rates mentioned because they vary from season to season and because every Florida golf resort offers packages that combine golf, accommodations, and amenities at a discount. Nobody should plan a golf vacation to Florida without thoroughly examining golf package possibilities.

11

After you read this book, the best place to continue your research is on the websites of the various resorts and destinations mentioned. Most websites give basic information on golf course offerings, and many feature golf package information. There's no need to pay inflated rack rates at golf resorts. Like a good golf package, this book will save you time and money.

Northwest

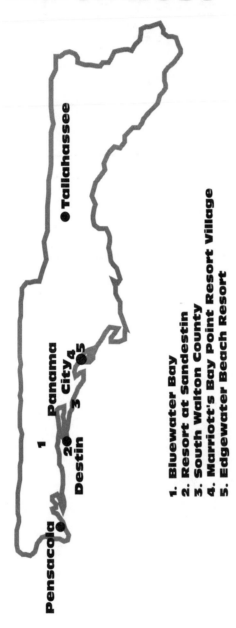

Tallahassee

Panama City

Destin

Pensacola

1. Bluewater Bay
2. Resort at Sandestin
3. South Walton County
4. Marriott's Bay Point Resort Village
5. Edgewater Beach Resort

Northwest

Bluewater Bay

ONE GETS THE SENSE that Marlin Perkins, Jane Goodall, and Tarzan and Jane might enjoy playing in a dream foursome at Bluewater Bay's two eighteen hole championship courses, which are sometimes junglelike, heavily wooded with pine, oak, and magnolia trees, and enhanced by marsh and water. Course designers Tom Fazio and Jerry Pate took full advantage of north Florida's natural elements—dense tree cover, rolling terrain, sandy soil, and a magnificent setting on the Choctawhatchee Bay. Fazio designed Bluewater Bay before he became a household name in the golf industry, and he did a masterful job with the low-lying ground, putting plenty of movement into the land with strategically placed mounding and bunkering.

The golf experience starts with play along the shoreline of the bay and moves through woodlands, followed by a journey through a pristine wetland area. Erratic and often strong winds blowing off the bay force golfers to put more thought than usual into club selection. If you lose concentration, swing the wrong club, and hit errant shots into the water or the tree cover, you're going to wish Tarzan was around to help you look for your lost golf balls.

Bluewater Bay's solution to help you lose fewer balls is the Bill Skelley School of Golf, which sets up shop at the resort from March through July and September through November for three- and five-day schools. Taught by a staff of professionals who have gone through a rigorous two-year training program, the curriculum's focus is on the mechanics of the swing rather than on the mental aspects of the game. High-speed, stop-action video analysis is used in conjunction with an instruction handbook and swing training aids.

Quiet and secluded, 1,800-acre Bluewater Bay is a resort/ residential community situated midway between Pensacola and Panama City. Accommodations range from studio units and town-house condominiums to patio homes and golf villas. Off the links, swimming, sailing, tennis, a private beach, and a fitness center head a long list of activities and amenities. The resort also has a 120-slip marina. For those who want to drop a line, the bay is an excellent spot to catch bass.

Bluewater Bay is a favorite getaway for active and retired military visitors, who take advantage of the numerous amenities (including golf) at Eglin Air Force Base, one of the nation's largest military bases, which is located ten miles from the resort.

Things to Know ▼ *Bluewater Bay*

Location ▼	1950 Bluewater Boulevard, Niceville (just north of Fort Walton Beach)
Phone ▼	(850) 897-3613, (800) 874-2128
Website ▼	www.bwbresort.com
Course ▼	Bluewater Bay Resort Course (36) – Tom Fazio, Jerry Pate
Major Amenities ▼	Three restaurants
▼	Nineteen tennis courts
▼	Four swimming pools
▼	120-slip on-site marina
▼	Bicycle rentals
Business Facilities ▼	Two meeting rooms with sixty-person capacity
Nearby Attractions ▼	Beach (15 miles away)
▼	Indian Temple Mound Museum
▼	Silver Sands Factory Stores in Destin

▲   ▲   ▲

Edgewater Beach Resort

IT MAY NOT BE the most prominent property on Florida's radar screen of golf resorts, but the Edgewater Beach Resort on Panama City Beach is rapidly gaining attention. Golfers relish its location— situated directly on what local tourism officials bill as "the world's most beautiful beach"— and its thirty-six holes of challenge and fun.

The 110-acre resort, overlooking the Gulf of Mexico's emerald green waters and snow white sands, has an on-site nine-hole executive course, which has nine small lakes and several island greens. The Edgewater also has a play agreement with the twenty-seven-hole Hombre Golf Club complex a few minutes away. One of the best courses in the Panhandle, the Hombre has hosted Nike Tour (now called the Buy.com Tour) events and recently served as a site for the First Stage PGA Tour Qualifying School. Weaving through wetlands, marshes, and lakes, the Hombre's fairways are rimmed with an assortment of palms, pines, and azaleas. Water comes into play on fifteen of the eighteen holes.

If you're lucky, you'll get to rub shoulders with a familiar pro golfer who serves as the Hombre's touring professional. Hubert Green, the 1977 U.S. Open champion and 1985 PGA Championship winner, does most of his practicing these days at the Hombre, where he prepares for his tournament schedule on the Senior PGA Tour. For those who want to swing like Green, the Hombre's Martin Green Golf Academy offers half-, two-, three-, and five-day schools featuring swing analysis.

The Edgewater is family-oriented: there's a sprawling pool with waterfalls and whirlpools, beach activities ranging from windsurfing to scuba diving, and an on-site Pizza Hut. The 550 suites in five Gulf-front towers and golf and tennis villas are roomy and family-friendly too: one-bedroom suites are 934 square feet; two-bedroom suites, 1,702 square feet; and three-bedroom suites, 1,928 square feet. One-, two-, and three-bedroom villas surround the par-3 executive course as well.

Things to Know ▼ *Edgewater Beach Resort*

Location ▼ 11212 Front Beach Road, Panama City Beach (20 miles from Panama City International Airport)

Phone ▼ (850) 235-4977, (800) 331-6338

Website ▼ www.edgewaterbeachresort.com

Courses ▼ The Hombre (18) – Wes Burnham

▼ Executive Course (9) – unknown

Major Amenities ▼ Beach

▼ Fitness center

▼ Ten tennis courts

▼ 11,000-square-foot free-form swimming pool

Business Facilities ▼ 32,700-square-foot conference center

Nearby Attractions ▼ Gulf World Marine Park

▼ Miracle Strip Amusement Park

▼ Shoppes at Edgewater (across the street)

▼ Ocean Opry Musical Revue

▲   ▲   ▲

Marriott's Bay Point Resort Village

STEP RIGHT UP, Mr. Low-handicapper! I've got one of Florida's toughest (and, yes, I'm including Bay Hill and the TPC Stadium Course in that comparison) golf courses waiting for you in Panama City Beach. The 6,885-yard Lagoon Legend Course at Marriott's Bay Point Resort Village is the number-one slope-rated course in the continental United States. With a 152 slope rating and 75.3 handicap rating, this water-laden gem is not recommended for the novice.

On the Lagoon Legend, designed by Bruce Devlin and Robert Von Hagge, water and marsh come into play on sixteen holes. The course is highlighted by three island greens that demand pinpoint-accurate approach shots or it's reach-for-the-ball-bag time. The eighteenth hole will leave a lasting impression of this layout: you shoot over a lagoon to an island and back over the water to the green.

If your confidence is destroyed by the perils of the Lagoon Legend, the resort's other course, the Willard Byrd–designed Meadows, has wider fairways and a bit less water. It also has a memorable finishing hole, a tricky dogleg right with five bunkers and a lake to the right of the green.

Rivaling golf for recreation supremacy at Bay Point is deep-sea fishing. A 205-slip marina borders the resort, providing easy access to the Gulf of Mexico and Intracoastal Waterway.

Between late May and October, blue and white marlin, sail-fish, yellowfin tuna, dolphin, and wahoo are prime targets for deep-sea charters, which can be arranged through the resort. Staged every July, the Bay Point Billfish Invitational, one of the nation's premier deep-sea fishing tournaments, features the largest purse ($483,000) in the continental United States. If you just want

Accurate approach shots, or else . . .

to drop a line in between rounds, you can cast from a 385-yard boardwalk with tackle obtained from Bay Point Guest Services.

For those looking to spin some fish stories or seeking to fondly remember (or forget) the Lagoon Legend, Stormy's Grille, overlooking the seventeenth tee, is generally regarded as one of the best restaurants in the Panama City Beach area. Besides prime steaks and local seafood grilled to personal request, Stormy's is famous for its martini bar.

Set on a 1,100-acre wildlife sanctuary overlooking St. Andrews Bay, Marriott's Bay Point Resort has 356 recently renovated rooms divided among the 200-room, Bermuda-style hotel and 156 one- and two-bedroom suites positioned along the resort grounds, gardens, and swimming pools.

Ahh, smooth greens and birdie putts.

Bay Point makes a strong effort to accommodate the entire family with a long list of amenities and activities. Several miles of biking/walking/jogging trails thread through the property, and a recreation center offers "night spiker" volleyball tournaments under the stars. Two family activities not to be missed are the dolphin excursions, which leave from Teddy's Pier every day, and beach bonfires, a nightly tradition where families and couples gather on the beach to make s'mores over a fire and watch the sunset.

Things to Know ▼ ***Marriott's Bay Point Resort***

Location ▼	4200 Marriott Drive, Panama City (bordered by Grand lagoon and St. Andrews Bay)
Phone ▼	(850) 236-6000, (800) 874-7105
Website ▼	www.marriottbaypoint.com
Courses ▼	Lagoon Legend (18) – Bruce Devlin, Robert Von Hagge
▼	Meadows (18) – Willard Byrd
Major Amenities ▼	Private beach
▼	Four swimming pools
▼	205-slip marina
▼	Seven restaurants and lounges
▼	Seasonal children's programs
▼	Tennis
▼	Walking/jogging trails
▼	Fitness center
Business Facilities ▼	40,000 square feet of meeting space
Nearby Attractions ▼	Gulf World Marine Park
▼	Miracle Strip Amusement Park
▼	Shell Island

▲   ▲   ▲

Resort at Sandestin

IF THE ONLY FISH you've been catching lately came from a restaurant menu, the 2,400-acre Resort at Sandestin is arguably the best place in Florida to combine a fishing/golf getaway.

The Resort at Sandestin is located eight miles east of Destin, a town boasting the title of "Sport Fishing Capital of the Gulf." And for good reason: more billfish, such as white and blue marlin, are brought into Destin each year than into all other Gulf fishing ports combined. With the largest charter boat fleet in Florida, you won't spend much time waiting for a ride. Anglers love the Destin area because they can reach deep water only ten miles from shore—the shortest distance in the Gulf—giving them more time to make the record catch and still fit in nine or eighteen holes each day. Adding to the angler appeal at the resort are a catch-and-release lake and dock- and fly-fishing lessons with resident expert Joy Dunlap.

Back on terra firma, the Resort at Sandestin's golf menu is equal to its world-class fishing opportunities. Four distinct championship golf courses—seventy-three holes in all—and a Golf Learning Center are the key components of the golf lifestyle at the resort.

The newest course, the Raven Golf Club, opened in 2000. Designed by Robert Trent Jones Jr., Raven has dramatic water features, wetlands, marshes, and thick stands of pine. For a seaside experience, the Links Course, designed by Tom Jackson, is a tough test, with water features on thirteen holes, including five alongside the massive Choctawhatchee Bay, and a strong, prevailing Gulf Coast wind that makes club selection difficult. High-handicappers might want to start out at Baytowne Golf Club, considered easier than the Links due to its wider fairways and fewer water hazards.

One of the big rewards for golfing guests at the Resort at Sandestin is access to the private Burnt Pine Golf Club, where a magnificent Rees Jones–designed course winds harmoniously through pristine northern Florida terrain. Featured in most national golf publication's top twenty-five courses in Florida, Burnt Pine is an attentively landscaped pallet of tumbling fairways, roller-coaster greens, and towering pine trees. The course's beauty is matched by its challenges: twelve holes require shots over water and every hole features strategic bunkering from tee to green. Burnt Pine opens with a few links-style holes, then turns into a marshy target layout.

Oceanside golf is as Floridian as suntans, theme parks, and pink flamingos.

If most of your fishing at the resort is confined to angling for golf balls in water hazards, help is available at the on-site Golf Learning Center headed by Tom Stickney, who uses biomechanical computer integration with split-screen video to record the movements of each student. Individual data is then compared to files and records of more than 200 PGA, Senior PGA and LPGA Tour professionals.

Every water sport imaginable is offered at the Resort at Sandestin as well as a putting course; tennis on hard, clay, and grass surfaces; a health club and day spa; an ocean sailing program; Jolee

Island Nature Conservatory; and thirty specialty shops. Guests have a wide range of accommodations in a 175-room inn as well as 740 rental units that include single-family and patio homes, and condominiums.

Things to Know ▼	***Resort at Sandestin***
Location ▼	9300 Highway 98, Destin (30 miles from Okaloosa Regional Airport)
Phone ▼	(850) 267-8150, (800) 622-1623
Website ▼	www.sandestin.com
Courses ▼	Raven Golf Club (18) – Robert Trent Jones Jr.
▼	Links Course (18) – Tom Jackson
▼	Baytowne Golf Club (18) – Tom Jackson
▼	Burnt Pine Golf Club (18) – Rees Jones
Major Amenities ▼	Seven miles of beach and bayfront
▼	Kidsail Sailing Academy
▼	Ocean School Sailing Program
▼	Fly-fishing lessons
▼	98-slip marina
▼	Health club
▼	Four swimming pools
▼	Thirteen tennis courts
▼	Award-winning Elephant Walk Restaurant
Business Facilities ▼	33,000 square feet of meeting space
Nearby Attractions ▼	Town of Seaside
▼	Silver Sands Factory Stores
▼	Grayton Beach State Recreation Area

▲   ▲   ▲

South Walton County

THE COMMAND, err, suggestion from your non-golfing spouse goes something like this: "Honey, let's find a place where we can hang out at the beach all day while you play golf." For any devout linkster who also treasures domestic bliss, the perfect beach/golf solution is South Walton County in the Panhandle near Destin. The twenty-six-mile stretch of dazzling white sand and clear turquoise Gulf of Mexico waters provides one of the state's longest stretches of unspoiled beaches. Enhancing the "life's a beach" lifestyle are quaint, walkable beach towns, pristine state parks with award-winning beaches, a wide variety of accommodations ranging from large homes and beach cottages to condos and hotel rooms, outlet shopping, and several excellent golf courses.

The heart and soul of the region is Seaside, a planned beach village inspired by Martha's Vineyard, Key West, Savannah, and other successful American coastal towns. The pedestrian-scaled streets are lined with ice cream–colored, Victorian-style cottages that have open porches, peaked tin roofs, and white picket fences. Dirt footpaths throughout Seaside are the main thoroughfares to the beach, providing a beach vacation that evokes memories of simpler times. Chances are, the only time you'll use your car is to drive to the golf course. Seaside has more than 250 cottages (one to six bedrooms) in its rental program, a bed-and-breakfast that offers fine dining, three swimming pools, six tennis courts, and a regulation croquet lawn. Down the sands a few miles, Rosemary Beach, another planned beach community, offers cottage rentals as well.

If you want a beach resort with on-site golf, the 120-unit Seascape Resort & Conference Center has one-, two-, and three-bedroom villas directly across from the Gulf and an eighteen-hole, par-71, 6,500-yard course with narrow, tree-lined fairways and expansive views. Other golf courses of note in the area include Emerald Bay Golf & Country Club, which has nine holes on Choctawhatchee Bay; Santa Rosa Golf & Beach Club, situated alongside the Gulf; and Wild Heron, where a new, Greg Norman–designed course named Shark's Tooth weaves through acres of preserved wetlands and around Lake Powell.

Surprisingly good golf opportunities are equaled by the area's surprisingly impressive dining scene. In the past few years, several excellent restaurants have opened to appease the large number of Atlanta fast-trackers who consider the area the ultimate getaway. Among the more celebrated possibilities are Chef Paul's at Carillon Beach, where Chef Paul Albrecht, formerly of Pano's and Paul's of Atlanta, offers a menu of seasonal fish; Café Thirty, which has an eclectic menu with a wood-fired rotisserie in a white-tablecloth setting; and Criolla's, a venerable favorite with innovative contemporary and Creole Caribbean cuisine.

Finally, no description of South Walton County would be complete without a mention of its world-class fishing grounds. There's freshwater, saltwater, bottom, offshore and surf fishing—whatever your pleasure. If you've got a fishing rod, by all means bring it.

Things to Know ▼ *South Walton County*

Location ▼	25 miles south of Interstate 10 between Okaloosa and Washington Counties
Phone ▼	(800) 622-1623 (Beaches of South Walton Tourist Development Council, P.O. Box 1248, Santa Rosa Beach 32459)
Website ▼	www.beachesofsouthwalton.com
Courses ▼	Emerald Bay (18) – Bob Cupp
▼	Shark's Tooth (18) – Greg Norman
▼	Santa Rosa (18) – Tom Jackson
▼	Seascape (18) – Joe Lee
Major Amenities ▼	Twenty-six miles of beaches
▼	Deep-sea fishing
▼	Diving
▼	Twenty-five mile bike trail
Business Facilities ▼	Hilton Sandestin Beach & Golf Resort
▼	Seascape
▼	Seaside
▼	Tops'l Beach & Racquet Resort
Nearby Attractions ▼	Eden State Gardens
▼	Grayton Beach State Recreation Area
▼	Silver Sands Outlet Mall

▲　　　▲　　　▲

Northeast

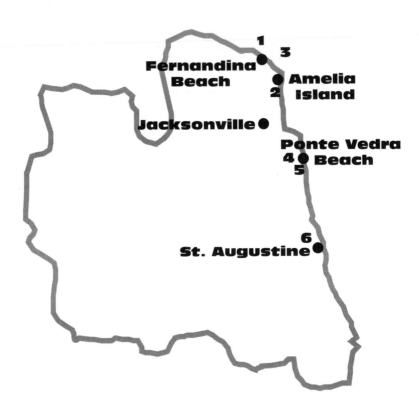

1 Fernandina Beach

3 Amelia Island

2

Jacksonville

Ponte Vedra
4 Beach
5

6
St. Augustine

1. Fernandina Beach
2. Ritz-Carlton, Amelia Island
3. Amelia Island Plantation Resort
4. Ponte Vedra Inn and Club
5. Sawgrass Marriott Resort
6. World Golf Village

Northeast

Amelia Island Plantation Resort

MASSIVE SAND DUNES framing sinewy fairways, tiny postage-stamp greens, crashing surf, and salty sea winds are an integral part of the golf experience at Amelia Island Plantation. Seven of the resort's fifty-four holes are situated directly on the Atlantic Ocean. Amelia Island Plantation has more seaside holes than any other resort in Florida.

There is water, water everywhere on the Ocean Links course, which has five holes along the Atlantic Shore and ten holes that feature lagoons and marsh wetlands. Unpredictable sea winds make the course even more difficult on some days, making club

selection a practice in calculated guesswork tantamount to answering
Regis Philbin's million-dollar question with no lifelines.

A round at the Long Point Club is an amazing trek through
a well-preserved wilderness area. The Tom Fazio–designed course
was carefully carved from the marshland and natural dune ridges
of the Intracoastal Waterway. Few resort courses in the United

Surf's up! Keep your drives off the beach.

States mold to the topography of the land like Long Point, where dense forests, fifty-foot-high sand dunes, and marsh and ocean views dominate the experience.

Nature lovers who come to Long Point had better have some game . . . or else. Golfers are required to hit a wide variety of shots, ranging from those over menacing marshlands to those aimed at narrow, tree-lined fairways and heavily duned, oceanside greens. Long Point is not a resort course designed to send high-handicappers back to their rooms with smiles. With its sometimes snaking, driveway-wide fairways and expansive, undulating greens, Long Point exposes imposters quickly and mercilessly.

The final member of the resort's championship trio is Oak Marsh. Appropriately named, the course meanders along saltmarsh creeks through moss-draped oaks. A classic Pete Dye design built in 1972, Oak Marsh has several Dye signature features, including long, contoured fairways and bulkheaded greens. Like all Dye courses, Oak Marsh demands accuracy and shot-making ability from its challengers. If you're a spray hitter off the tee, be prepared for the nature walk of your life as you roam the fairway fringes to locate your ball.

The 1,350-acre Amelia Island Plantation Resort is a symphony of oaks, palmettos, sand dunes, sea oats, and large lagoons situated on the southern end of a thirteen-mile-long barrier island thirty miles northeast of Jacksonville. Two types of accommodations are available: the Amelia Inn & Beach Club has 249 hotel rooms with private balconies facing the ocean; the Villas of Amelia features 418 ocean- and resort-view hotel rooms as well as one-, two-, three- and four-bedroom villas with kitchen facilities, dining areas, and private bedrooms.

Things to Know ▼ *Amelia Island Plantation*

Location ▼	4700 Amelia Island Parkway, Amelia Island (30 miles northeast of Jacksonville International Airport)
Phone ▼	(888) 261-6161
Website ▼	www.aipfl.com
Courses ▼	Ocean Links (18) – Bobby Weed, Pete Dye
▼	Long Point Club (18) – Tom Fazio
▼	Oak Marsh (18) – Pete Dye
Major Amenities ▼	Twenty-three tennis courts
▼	Spa
▼	Fitness center
▼	Swimming pools
▼	Horseback riding
▼	Biking
▼	Deep-sea fishing
Business Facilities ▼	50,000 square feet of meeting space
Nearby Attractions ▼	Fernandina Beach historic district
▼	Fort Clinch State Park
▼	Amelia Lighthouse
▼	Amelia Village shopping complex

▲   ▲   ▲

Fernandina Beach

FERNANDINA BEACH, a coastal village on Amelia Island, is rarely, if ever, mentioned when Florida's top golf destinations are being discussed. Yet with a fabulous historic district, several charming bed-and-breakfasts, and a superb public golf course minutes from downtown, the town is a great destination for golfers and non-golfing spouses seeking something different in a golf getaway.

About a five-minute drive from downtown Fernandina Beach, the twenty-seven-hole Fernandina Beach Golf Club is one of the finest municipal golf facilities in the Southeast. Designed in the mid-1950s, the North and West nines are comprised of wide fairways lined with live oaks, pines, and palms along with small, elevated greens guarded by bunkers. Be prepared to air out your driver on the second hole on the West Course, a par-5, 613-yard slight dogleg left. Built in the mid-1970s, the South Course has more water hazards and woods of magnolia and hickory. The complex includes putting and chipping greens, a driving range, and pro shop.

Dating back to the 1850s, Fernandina Beach was once a vibrant Victorian seaport and later the birthplace of the modern shrimping industry. Today more than fifty blocks of the downtown area are lined with nineteenth-century Victorian homes whose architectural styles range from Queen Anne and Chinese Chippendale to "Mississippi Steamboat." Among the notable inns in or near the town center are the Addison House, an 1876 house that has five guest chambers with private baths and fireplaces and nine rooms with whirlpools and private porches; the Bailey House, an 1895 Queen Anne–style Victorian inn listed on the National Register of Historic Places, with a grand staircase, stained-glass windows, working marble fireplaces, and authentic Victorian antiques; and Florida House Inn, built in 1857 and reputedly the state's oldest surviving tourist hotel, with a guest registry that includes such famous historical figures as Cuban revolutionary José Martí and Ulysses S. Grant.

Off-the-course entertainment begins and ends on Fernandina Beach's Centre Street, which has an eclectic assortment of curios, antique shops, restaurants, and taverns. The best place to cool off after a toasty day on the links is the 123-year-old Palace Saloon, Florida's oldest tavern. The former haunt of the Vanderbilts, DuPonts, and Carnegies still serves drinks from a forty-foot mahogany bar.

Things to Know ▼ *Fernandina Beach*

Location ▼	Amelia Island (30 miles northeast of Jacksonville International Airport)
Phone ▼	(904) 277-0717, (800) 2AMELIA (Amelia Island Tourist Development Council)
Website ▼	www.ameliaisland.org
Course ▼	Fernandina Beach Golf Club (27) – Ed Matteson, Tommy Birdsong
Major Amenities ▼	Centre Street shopping district
	▼ Victorian homes district
	▼ Fort Clinch State Park
	▼ Numerous bed-and-breakfasts
Business Facilities ▼	Available at nearby resorts Amelia Island Plantation and Ritz-Carlton, Amelia Island
Nearby Attractions ▼	Amelia Island Lighthouse
	▼ Fernandina Harbor

▲　　　▲　　　▲

Ponte Vedra Inn & Club

ONE OF FLORIDA'S golf resort forefathers, the venerable Ponte Vedra Inn & Club opened in 1928. Outwardly, the 300-acre resort, located twenty-two miles southeast of Jacksonville, has always retained an all-Florida look, with its manicured lawns dotted with palms and bright flowers set against an Atlantic Ocean backdrop. A step into its old lobby, however, revealed an ambience more reminiscent of the Ivy League than the Sunshine State.

The Inn & Club traces its Ivy League roots back to the late 1930s, when one of its original planners, a Princeton graduate, put out a call to his former classmates to become members and a large number responded. A cursory glance at the first hotel guest registers reveals a significant number of visitors from social hubs like Grosse Pointe, Michigan; Newport , Rhode Island; and Greenwich, Connecticut.

The original, clubby, New England–style main lodge was recently replaced with a new, four-story structure designed with an old-Florida architectural theme. Today guests walk into a bright and airy two-story lobby with pine flooring; an exposed cypress, coffered ceiling; a massive chandelier; a sweeping staircase; and European-style guest registration desks. Enhancing the modernization are several luxury retail stores and specialty shops. The second and third floors have twenty guest rooms accented with Queen Anne–style furniture. A 1,200-square-foot Presidential Suite occupies the fourth floor.

Like the resort itself, the two golf courses have undergone several facelifts in their long history. In the late 1920s, British architect Herbert Bertram Strong used more than one hundred mules on the Ocean Course to shape contours, dredge lagoons, and build up a series of earthen mounds that dot fairways, creating dramatic undulations. Redesigned by Robert Trent Jones Sr. in 1947 and again in 1998 by Bobby Weed, the course has an island hole just like that of its neighbor course a few miles away, the TPC Stadium Course at Sawgrass. Speculation has it that the Ocean's island hole was the inspiration for Pete Dye's famous seventeenth hole at the Stadium Course.

The Lagoon Course's first nine holes, designed by Robert Trent Jones Sr., opened in 1961, with the second nine, a Joe Lee design, debuting in 1977. A shotmaker's delight, the Lagoon layout is a mosaic of lakes and lagoons that come into play on eleven holes, accented by small, well-bunkered greens that place a premium on accurate approach shots.

No doubt, the Ponte Vedra Inn & Club pays homage to tradition, but it has not been blinded to today's pampering resort lifestyle. Heading the list of amenities are a golf academy, European-style spa, 4,000-square-foot fitness center, and a private beach. Ponte Vedra's signature dining experience is the Seafoam Room, which has candlelit tables and tri-level seating affording every diner a spectacular view of the Atlantic Ocean. Most of the resort's 221 rooms and suites have balconies or patios overlooking the Atlantic. In addition, there are golf cottages featuring fireplaces and balconies or patios.

Things to Know ▼	*Ponte Vedra Inn & Club*
Location ▼	200 Ponte Vedra Boulevard, Ponte Vedra Beach (20 miles southeast of Jacksonville)
Phone ▼	(904) 285-1111, (800) 234-7842
Website ▼	www.pvresorts.com
Courses ▼	Ocean Course (18) – Robert Trent Jones Sr., Herbert Bertram Strong, Bobby Weed
▼	Lagoon Course (18) – Robert Trent Jones Sr., Bobby Weed
Major Amenities ▼	Spa
▼	Golf academy
▼	Four swimming pools
▼	Fitness center
▼	Tennis courts
Business Facilities ▼	30,000 square feet of meeting space
Nearby Attractions ▼	St. Augustine
▼	St. Johns Landing Shopping Complex
▼	World Golf Village

▲   ▲   ▲

Ritz-Carlton, Amelia Island

THE RITZ-CARLTON, Amelia Island must surely have a Jack Nicklaus–size trophy case. The ten-year-old, opulent, oceanside resort consistently receives the prestigious AAA Five Diamond Award and the Mobil Travel Guide Four-Star Rating and recently was selected the eighth best U.S. resort by the Zagat Survey. Even the most discerning, demanding traveler would have a difficult time finding fault with any aspect of the Ritz-Carlton, Amelia Island.

Walk a few steps into the Ritz's elegant lobby and you're surrounded by expensive furnishings, fresh flowers, and an attentive staff that inquires more about your every need than a mother doting on a five-year-old. At the Ritz, ask once and your request receives immediate attention—no exceptions.

Skirting the hotel is the Golf Club of Amelia Island course, a Mark McCumber/Gene Littler design that hosted the 1998 Senior Liberty Mutual Legends of Golf. The opening nine holes wind through centuries-old oaks and towering pines, while water and marshes dominate the back nine. You absolutely must hit consistently straight tee shots, because the landing areas aren't very wide and the marshland will gobble balls up faster than one of those tractors at a driving range.

Following a round of golf, the lobby is a wonderful place to luxuriate with a cool libation. Panoramic views of the resort's verdant gardens, rolling sand dunes, and the Atlantic Ocean beyond provide inspiration and photo opportunities. Not surprisingly, some golfers have trouble motivating themselves to leave the ultra-plush, pampering confines of the hotel. All 449 rooms and suites have private balconies overlooking the Atlantic Ocean, marble baths, goose-down pillows, fluffy bathrobes, European toiletries, and a high-speed Internet service. Guests in one of the sixty-two Club-floor rooms enjoy a concierge staff and a private, fireplaced lounge where cocktails and beverages are served throughout the day.

When it's time to dine, the place for Amelia Island residents and guests to see and be seen is the Ritz's luxurious restaurant, the Grill. Regarded by several food critics as one of the best restaurants in Florida, the Grill's fare consists of fresh seafood, meats, and wild game flown in from all over the world.

Things to Know ▼	*Ritz Carlton, Amelia Island*
Location ▼	4750 Amelia Island Parkway, Amelia Island (30 miles northeast of Jacksonville International Airport)
Phone ▼	(904) 277-1100, (800) 241-3333
Website ▼	www.ritzcarlton.com
Course ▼	Golf Club of Amelia Island (18) – Mark McCumber, Gene Littler
Major Amenities ▼	Three restaurants
▼	Nine-court tennis complex
▼	Fitness center
▼	Indoor pool with whirlpool
▼	Outdoor pool
▼	Full-service beauty salon
▼	Ritz Kids program
▼	Internet and computer assistance
Business Facilities ▼	32,000 square feet of meeting space
Nearby Attractions ▼	Village of Fernandina Beach
▼	Fort Clinch State Park
▼	Amelia Island Lighthouse

▲   ▲   ▲

Sawgrass Marriott Resort

It doesn't have an imposing marketing moniker that mentions a monster or ferocious animal, yet the somewhat generically named TPC at Sawgrass Stadium Course at Sawgrass Marriott Resort in Ponte Vedra Beach is one of the most feared courses in the world. If you play only one course in Florida, make it this one—an in-your-face challenge in which every shot requires patience, daring, and skill.

The Stadium Course gets its name from its unique "built-in" spectator bleachers. Narrow fairways—some not much wider than a two-car driveway—are lined with immense waste bunkers, grassy mounds and knolls, and pool table–fast greens. Designed by Pete Dye, the course is the site of the PGA Tour's Players Championship and is universally regarded as one of the most difficult layouts on the tour schedule.

Many golfers who aren't aware of the Stadium's history are surprised to learn the current version is actually a kinder, gentler design compared to the original, which debuted in 1980. Back then, one high-profile tour pro who played the course referred to Dye as "diabolical." Dye eventually altered the design of some holes, making it more playable for the pros. However, high-handicappers still find the course to be one of the toughest courses anywhere. To do well, repeat this mantra: "I must play from the correct tee." If you don't, you might never finish your round.

The Stadium's most famous and often photographed hole is the par-3 seventeenth island hole, where many a golfer has lost balls in the water as well as any hope of a low-scoring round. With a green accessible only by a narrow walkway, golfers must hit 132

For a splashingly good time, try the #17 Island hole at the TPC Stadium Course.

yards over a lagoon into a stiff Atlantic breeze. If the course isn't crowded, you get two shots at the green—then it's drop time.

While the Stadium Course is undoubtedly the lead entrée, the golf menu at Sawgrass Marriott Resort is a lengthy one, with a total of ninety-nine holes of golf. The other courses are the TPC at Sawgrass Valley Course, a water-happy layout crafted by Pete Dye and Jerry Pate; Sawgrass Country Club, a twenty-seven-hole complex designed by Ed Seay, with several oceanside fairways; Marsh Landing Country Club, a Seay design that weaves through pockets of intracoastal marshes and lagoons; and Oak Bridge Club Course, a short, tight Seay creation.

For an after-the-round (or, in some cases, postmortem) celebration, the dining equivalent of the Stadium Course is the Augustine Grille, an elegant, private clubhouse-style room appointed with rich mahogany, imported Belgian linen, and pine green walls dotted with paintings of some the world's most famous golf holes. Chef Tony Pels, who honed his craft at Spago in Los Angeles and Citronelle in Baltimore, provides an exciting, eclectic, contemporary menu.

The hotel, with its seventy-foot-high atrium, towering palm trees, rock carvings, and cascading waterfalls, is one of the most welcoming in the state and the centerpiece of the sprawling 4,800-acre resort/residential community that is peppered with lagoons and groves of giant live oaks, magnolias, and palms. Included in the 508-unit inventory are 324 water-view guest rooms, 24 suites, and 160 golf villas.

Smooth sailing on and off the course at Sawgrass.

Things to Know ▼ *Sawgrass Marriott Resort*

Location ▼	1000 PGA Tour Boulevard, Ponte Vedra Beach (20 miles southeast of Jacksonville)
Phone ▼	(800) 457-4653
Website ▼	www.marriotthotels.com/JAXSW
Courses ▼	TPC at Sawgrass Stadium Course (18) – Pete Dye
▼	TPC at Sawgrass Valley Course (18) – Pete Dye, Jerry Pate
▼	Sawgrass Country Club (27) – Ed Seay
▼	Marsh Landing Country Club (18) – Ed Seay
▼	Oak Bridge Club Course (18) – Ed Seay
Major Amenities ▼	Six restaurants and two lounges
▼	Three swimming pools
▼	Grasshopper Gang Children's Club
▼	Private Atlantic Ocean beach
▼	Seventeen tennis courts
▼	Fitness facilities and massage therapy
▼	Horseback riding and biking trails
▼	Boutique shopping
Business Facilities ▼	46,000 square feet of meeting space
Nearby Attractions ▼	St. Augustine
▼	World Golf Village
▼	Jacksonville Landing shopping complex
▼	Jacksonville Zoological Gardens
▼	Marineland

▲   ▲   ▲

World Golf Village

BASEBALL HAS COOPERSTOWN, New York. Football has Canton, Ohio. Basketball has Springfield, Massachusetts. When fans of America's major sports pay homage to their heroes and traditions, they congregate in these revered towns. Golf enthusiasts meet at the World Golf Village, a 6,300-acre resort/residential golf community near St. Augustine. Home to the World Golf Hall of Fame, the World Golf Village encompasses golf facilities, accommodations, a shopping marketplace with one of the world's largest golf stores, a golf library and resource center, a PGA Tour Golf Academy, PGA Tour Productions, and other amenities.

If your image of a sports museum is a dark edifice where bronze plaques and static displays abound, you will need to readjust your thinking at the World Golf Hall of Fame. Combining a Disneyesque flair for entertainment and cutting-edge design, the exhibits in this museum appeal to casual observers as well as golf fanatics. More than seventy major exhibits and displays celebrate the game. Visitors can walk across a replica of the famous Swilcan Burn Bridge from the eighteenth hole on the Old Course at St. Andrews, putt with an antique putter, travel back to golf's golden era at one of the museum's mini-theaters, or watch a film at the IMAX theater. Interspersed throughout is an eclectic collection of artifacts, including Jack Nicklaus' favorite fly-fishing rod, astronaut Alan Shepherd's "lunar club" from the 1971 Apollo 14 mission to the moon, a pair of Dwight Eisenhower's golf shoes and socks, and a golf-related etching by Rembrandt. Tiger Woods and Nancy Lopez are among the contemporary players who provide commentary via hand-held Acousticguides.

Adjacent to the World Golf Hall of Fame is the World Golf Village Renaissance Resort, a sleek, ten-story hotel with an atrium lobby that is appointed with lush, tropical foliage and towering palm trees. Most of the 300 guest rooms have a balcony with a view of the Village. The other on-site accommodation is the 102-villa Vistana Resort, which has one-and two-bedroom units ranging in size from 650 to 1,500 square feet.

The ultimate golf lifestyle at World Golf Village.

Beyond the excitement of the Hall of Fame, playing golf on great courses is an important part of the World Golf Village experience. In recent years, few courses in Florida have received as much attention and publicity as the Village's The King & The Bear course, the only design collaboration by golf icons Arnold Palmer and Jack Nicklaus. Between them, Arnie and Jack have designed more than 400 courses worldwide, but this is the only one they have worked on together.

High weeds, bunkers, water. . . . Can you say "bogey time"?

Opened in November 2000, the course has more of a Nicklaus influence. Arnie's design team handled the original routing, and Jack's group formulated the strategy of the course and bunker placement. Among the more intriguing features are the beach bunkers, massive sandy fairway hazards spilling into the adjoining lakes without a lip, just like a beach. A stern test from the championship tees, the course invites all comers with five well-spaced sets of tees and multiple choices for women.

Golf legends Sam Snead and Gene Sarazen served as consultants to designer Bobby Weed on the Village's first course, the Slammer and Squire, which debuted in 1998. The PGA Tour Golf Academy, the only golf school in the world with the PGA Tour brand, is headed by Scott Sackett, a Golf Magazine Top 100 teacher, and Calvin Peete, a twelve-time winner on the PGA Tour who also serves as the academy's resident tour instructor. For fans of the 1980 comedy Caddyshack, the Murray Bros. Caddyshack restaurant on the Walk of Champions at World Golf Village is a must-see. The fun, family-style restaurant seats 300 and has a casual, golf-themed menu including "sand-wedges" (sandwiches) and "slices" (side dishes).

Things to Know ▼	*World Golf Village*
Location ▼	21 World Golf Place, St. Augustine (Exit 95-A off I 95)
Phone ▼	(904) 940-4000, (800) 948-4746
Website ▼	www.wgv.com
Courses ▼	The King & The Bear (18) – Arnold Palmer, Jack Nicklaus
▼	Slammer & Squire (18) – Sam Snead, Gene Sarazen
Major Amenities ▼	On-site shopping village
▼	31,000-square-foot PGA Tour Stop retail store
▼	Murray Bros. Caddyshack
▼	Eighteen-hole putting green
▼	132-yard island challenge hole
▼	Walk of Champions
Business Facilities ▼	76,000 square feet of meeting space
Nearby Attractions ▼	St. Augustine
▼	Beaches
▼	Deep-sea fishing
▼	St. Augustine Outlet Center

▲   ▲   ▲

Central

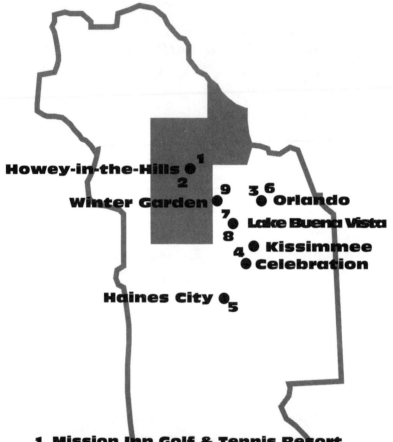

Howey-in-the-Hills ● 1
　　　　　　　　　　2
Winter Garden ● 　9　3 6
　　　　　　　　　　● Orlando
　　　　　　　　7
　　　　　　　　● Lake Buena Vista
　　　　　　　8
　　　　　　　4 ● Kissimmee
　　　　　　　● Celebration

Haines City ● 5

1. Mission Inn Golf & Tennis Resort
2. Lake County (shaded)
3. Arnold Palmer's Bay Hill Club & Lodge
4. ChampionsGate
5. Grenelefe Golf & Tennis Resort
6. Grand Cypress Resort
7. Walt Disney World
8. Orlando World Center Marriott
9. Orange County National Golf Center & Lodge

Central

Arnold Palmer's Bay Hill Club & Lodge

IN THE WORD-ASSOCIATION GAME, Bay Hill is synonymous with Arnold Palmer. While Tiger Woods may be the newly anointed prince of professional golf, Palmer is indisputably the King. Every March, Palmer, a part-time resident at Bay Hill, hosts the Bay Hill Invitational, which attracts one of the strongest fields on the PGA Tour. From Woods and Mickelson to Norman and Nicklaus, everyone comes to Bay Hill to honor "Arnie."

Nestled in a splendidly landscaped residential community in southwest Orlando, Bay Hill is a private club with a twenty-seven-hole golf complex. There are five ways you can play Bay Hill:

be a member, be a guest of a member, be a friend of Arnie's, be a PGA Tour pro playing in the tournament, or (the most likely) stay as a guest at the lodge that overlooks the number nine green. Visitors and members can play twenty-seven holes—the original eighteen plus the Charger nine, arranged as separate nine-hole layouts. The Charger nine is similar in design to the original.

The par-72, 7,114-yard course definitely has Palmer's stamp on it. He first encountered the course in 1965 during an exhibition match with Jack Nicklaus. Smitten by Dick Wilson's design and the surrounding terrain, Palmer immediately began pursuing its purchase. He and several associates took over a lease on the property in 1970, exercising a purchase option in 1976.

Bay Hill reflects the personality of Palmer, one of the modern era's most daring and aggressive players. The course, which sweeps along the shores of the Butler Chain of Lakes, is long and tight. Most of the toughest par-4 holes play into a prevailing north wind, encouraging the hard, low tee shot that is Palmer's trademark. When the holes dogleg, most of them turn from right to left, favoring his preferred flight pattern, a draw.

The most talked-about holes are the final two. The seventeenth is a 219-yard par-3 with a large green protected by water and treacherous pin positions. One of the best finishing holes on the PGA Tour, the eighteenth, a 441-yard, par-4 dogleg, has been called many things by players (a great number of them unprintable). For birdie, you must hit a laser-accurate mid-iron shot over water to a huge, undulating green bordered by deep bunkers on the left side. More than a few players simply lay up on their second shot, sacrificing hero status for a chance to make par.

The sixty-four-room lodge at the Bay Hill Club is a throwback to a time when private clubs offered comfortable on-site accommodations for guests. Keeping with Palmer's low-key personality, the design and ambience of the lodge are unpretentious and relaxing.

Guests at the lodge are treated as club members, not as interlopers. Better still, the friendly and approachable Palmer retains a strong presence at the club and often chats with guests on the course and in the dining room.

Things to Know ▼ *Arnold Palmer's Bay Hill*

Location ▼	Southwest quadrant of the city; 9000 Bay Hill Boulevard, Orlando
Phone ▼	(407) 876-2429, (888) 422-9445
Website ▼	www.bayhill.com
Courses ▼	Challenger (9) – Dick Wilson, Arnold Palmer
▼	Champion (9) – Dick Wilson, Arnold Palmer
▼	Charger (9) – Arnold Palmer, Ed Seay
Major Amenities ▼	Swimming pool
▼	Tennis courts
▼	Two restaurants
Business Facilities ▼	5,355 square feet of meeting space
Nearby Attractions ▼	Universal Studios
▼	Sea World
▼	Walt Disney World

▲　　　▲　　　▲

Celebration

CELEBRATION, A CONCEPT TOWN near Orlando, was artfully developed by the Disney Company to emulate a small Southern town with pre-1940s' architecture. A pedestrian-friendly environment set on 4,900 acres, the town has a central core with shops, restaurants, a bank, a movie theater, a hotel, and a golf course. For Disney fans enamored of the cleanliness and orderliness of the theme parks, Celebration has impeccable landscaping at every turn and not a piece of litter anywhere. Ditto for the golf course.

Remindful of the village layout of St. Andrews in Scotland, the daily-fee golf course was integrated into the land plan and serves as a focal point of the community. A design collaboration by Robert Trent Jones Sr. and Robert Trent Jones Jr., the course is surrounded by natural wetlands. Unlike many courses with individual, tree-lined fairways, the Celebration Golf Club has periodic clusters of native oak, pine, and magnolia trees, which enhance a parklike ambience.

Much like Disney's theme parks, the Celebration Golf Club appeals to patrons of all ages. There are five sets of tees on the eighteen-hole championship layout as well as generously wide fairways and open-entry greens on many holes, which make the course enjoyable for all skill levels. Be aware, however, the course is no pushover, especially from the 6,786-yard back tees. Celebration hosted the 1999 Oldsmobile Scramble Finals and the 1999 USGA Senior Amateur Qualifier.

While many courses give only lip service to junior golfers, Celebration embraces Tiger wannabes. Its innovative, three-hole junior course, which is maintained to professional tourlike standards, costs only $1 for kids to play. Parents are not allowed access unless accompanied by a youngster. In addition, Celebration is a Nike

Golf Learning Center, offering a variety of schools and camps. Headquarters for instruction and for post-round libations, burgers, and salads is Celebration's classy, high-roofed, one-story, 16,500-square-foot clubhouse, which blends admirably with the community's homes and townhomes.

Three blocks from the golf course, the 115-room Celebration Hotel, which sits on the shore of Celebration's lake at the end of the town's public esplanade, is an exceptional boutique hotel. Incorporating 1920's coastal architecture, the wood-frame structure is conveniently located within 100 yards or so of four fine-dining restaurants, shops, and a two-screen movie theater. For those seeking a haven to drown their sorrows or to toast a great round on the links, the hotel's elegant lobby, with its small bar, piano and lake view, is a wonderful spot. Golfers can travel to the golf course in the hotel's black 1947 Cadillac.

Most of the guest rooms at the Celebration Hotel offer a

Celebration Hotel, a welcome reprieve after a day on the links.

lakeside view, and those located on the first floor have twelve-foot ceilings. The recreation amenity lineup is astounding for a boutique hotel. On-site are a heated outdoor pool, Jacuzzi, and fitness room. Hotel guests may also use the 60,000 square-foot Celebration Health and Wellness Center.

Things to Know ▼	*Celebration*
Location ▼	US 192 East in Kissimmee
	700 Bloom Street, Celebration (hotel)
Phone ▼	(407) 566-4653 (golf)
▼	(407) 566-6000 (hotel)
Website ▼	www.celebrationgolf.com
Course ▼	Celebration Golf Club (18) – Robert Trent Jones Sr., Robert Trent Jones Jr.
Major Amenities ▼	Health and wellness center
▼	Shopping district
▼	Movie theater
▼	Four restaurants
Business Facilities ▼	5,000 square feet of meeting space
Nearby Attractions ▼	Walt Disney World resort
▼	Water Mania Water Park
▼	Old Town shopping complex

▲   ▲   ▲

ChampionsGate

WHAT DO YOU GET when you team one of the world's most famous golf course designers with arguably the world's best and most well known golf instructors? The answer is ChampionsGate, a sprawling, 1,400-acre, $800-million golf resort three miles west of Walt Disney World. ChampionsGate sports two eighteen-hole courses designed by Greg Norman and the headquarters facility for the David Leadbetter Golf Academies.

Set in one of Orlando's most dynamic growth areas, ChampionsGate is located within a few miles of Celebration, the Disney Company's master planned town. In fact, ChampionsGate has a grandiose, Disneyesque scale to its plan, which includes a 20,000-square-foot clubhouse with panoramic views of both golf courses and a 732-room Omni Orlando Resort hotel with a spa and multiple restaurants expected to open in late 2002.

Most golf fans are familiar with Greg Norman, the golfer (a.k.a. the "Shark"), but Greg Norman, the course designer, is at the top of his game as well. A winner of seventy-five professional tournaments, Norman has designed more than thirty courses, including Sugarloaf Country Club near Atlanta, Georgia; the Medalist Club in Hobe Sound, Florida; and The Great White Course at Doral Golf Resort & Spa in Miami.

The Shark's two ChampionsGate courses are superb additions to his designer resumé. The International Course, a links-style layout, has rectangular tee boxes, sandy dunes, and pot bunkers as well as hard-and-fast playing surfaces reminiscent of the great old courses of the British Isles. The National Course is a traditional, parklike course carved from 200 acres of citrus groves and natural Florida forest. Norman did a masterful job of sculpting the pancake-flat central Florida terrain into links-style courses. The brilliant green, carpetlike fairways are framed by the stark, unfinished look of brown dunes and moguls. There are several pot bunkers, but the course has no conventional hazards of sand-filled bunkers.

Instantly joining courses like Bay Hill, Lake Nona, and Isleworth as one of Orlando's most challenging tracks, the International has made a quick ascent in Florida's course rankings. Playing to 7,381 yards from the championship tees, the International is a formidable challenge. Low-handicappers and those who can hit straight tee shots will find the course difficult but thoroughly enjoyable. However, for those who play only a few times a year and insist on playing the back tees, get ready for some "snowmen" dotting your scorecard.

Somewhat less difficult, the National presumably serves as a playable option for the less serious players in the name-tag set attending meetings and conferences at the Omni Resort. Playing to 7,195 yards from the back tees, the National is no pushover but it does offer long, narrow greens, many of which are open in front for run-up shots. Some holes have bunkers in front and at the sides but never behind.

For those with swing flaws that prevent good play on either course, help is not far away. The David Leadbetter Academy is on the opposite end of the resort's expansive practice range. Amenities at the complex include spacious classrooms, student relaxation areas, a pro shop, a video and computer analysis area, a 65,000-square-foot lesson tee, two indoor Swing Solutions swing analysis units and four portable units for use on the practice tee, a short game practice area, and a master club fitter with an on-site shop.

Things to Know ▼	*ChampionsGate*
Location ▼	1400 Masters Boulevard, ChampionsGate (Exit 24 from I-4)
Phone ▼	(407) 787-4653, (888) 558-9301
Website ▼	www.championsgategolf.com
Courses ▼	International Course (18) – Greg Norman
▼	National Course (18) – Greg Norman
Major Amenities ▼	David Leadbetter Golf Academy
Business Facilities ▼	70,000 square feet of business space at the Omni Orlando Resort
Nearby Attractions ▼	Walt Disney World
▼	Celebration
▼	Sea World

▲   ▲   ▲

Grand Cypress Resort

IMAGINE PLAYING a golf course set in an open meadow with deep pot bunkers, bridges, stone walls, and long grassy mounds. Now imagine that course in Florida. The Jack Nicklaus–designed, eighteen-hole New Course at the Grand Cypress Resort in Orlando has been a hit in the land of palmetto and palm trees since opening in 1988. Inspired by the Old Course at St. Andrews, considered by many to be the birthplace of golf, the New Course pays homage to the great courses of Scotland. By careful and thoughtful design, Nicklaus has transported a slice of the Scottish links to central Florida.

Golfers familiar with St. Andrews will notice a number of similarities between the Scottish course and New Course. A creek that fronts the first green on New Course is similar to the Swilcan Burn at St. Andrews. The seventeenth hole at New Course resembles St. Andrews' famous Road Hole, and the fifth hole, with its bunkers on the right side of the fairway, is similar to the Principal's Nose and Deacon Sime at St. Andrews. New Course's remaining holes incorporate key design elements of the legendary Scottish course.

Lending an air of authenticity to New Course are replicas of St. Andrews' stone bridges and walls, a snaking burn (creek), a starter's hut overlooking the first tee, seven double greens, five-foot flag pins, deep pot bunkers (some as deep as twelve feet) with ladders, and simple white fences. If you want to score well, you're best to have a bunker shot in your arsenal. The course has some 140 bunkers—the ninth hole alone has 21. There are few trees in the interior of the course, however, and water comes into play on only seven holes. Nicklaus gives golfers many options to bump and run shots, which can help scoring on a windy course.

Interestingly, the resort does not overseed the fairways on New Course during winter months, which causes them to turn brown in an impressive resemblance of St. Andrews. When the wind blows hard during January, February, and March in central Florida, golfers can immerse themselves even deeper in a Scottish links dream. To fully capture the ambience of St. Andrews, golfers have the option of walking New Course. The resort's other course, the twenty-seven-hole Grand Cypress course, comprises three nines, the North, South, and East. All play to par-36 and feature terraced fairways and platform greens. Nicklaus has added some Scottish elements to these nines as well, with long grass and wildflowers, which create a Scottish glen effect.

A watery grave where all bad golf shots go to rest in peace.

For those in search of a swing tune-up or even a complete overhaul, the on-site Grand Cypress Academy of Golf is one of the most innovative golf instructional facilities in the nation. Instructors use the science of biomechanics, with video and computer swing analysis and techniques, to help improve performance.

Within walking distance of the Academy and framing some of the golf holes at the 1,500-acre resort is the Villas of Grand Cypress, a Mediterranean-style complex. Its 146 one- to four-bedroom suites, ranging in size from 650 to 3,300 square feet, have patios and verandas. Less than five minutes away via shuttle is the 750-room Hyatt Regency, which has commanding views of a twenty-one-acre lake with 1,000 feet of white-sand beach.

Things to Know ▼ *Grand Cypress Resort*

Location ▼	One North Jacaranda, Orlando
Phone ▼	(407) 239-4700, (800) 835-7377
Website ▼	www.grandcypress.com
Courses ▼	New Course (18) – Jack Nicklaus
▼	Grand Cypress (27) – Jack Nicklaus
Major Amenities ▼	Grand Cypress Academy of Golf
▼	Equestrian center
▼	Twelve tennis courts
▼	Spa
▼	Nature and exercise trails
Business Facilities ▼	7,000 square feet of meeting space at Grand Cypress Resort, 65,000 square feet at Hyatt Regency
Nearby Attractions ▼	Downtown Disney shopping and dining complex
▼	Walt Disney World
▼	Sea World
▼	Discovery Cove

▲   ▲   ▲

Grenelefe Golf & Tennis Resort

CARVED FROM FORMER CITRUS groves and ranch land on the shores of Lake Marion, Grenelefe provides three excellent golf courses with few distractions. Grenelefe, a peaceful, self-contained, resort/residential community, gives you a definite sense of isolation even though the resort is only a thirty-five-minute drive from downtown Orlando.

Surprisingly, the terrain at Grenelefe has a much more woodsy environment than one would associate with land formerly used for agricultural purposes. The resort's 800 villas are nestled amid beautiful oak trees and flower-laden common areas. All of the villas have private, outside entrances, and the one- and two-bedroom units have full living and dining rooms and kitchens with all the amenities of home.

Each of Grenelefe's three courses was designed by a different architect. The headliner layout is the Robert Trent Jones Sr.–designed West Course, one of the state's longest courses. Consistently rated as one of the top ten courses in Florida, the West Course has been a regular site for the PGA Tour Qualifying Finals in recent years. A traditional layout, the course has long, tight, rolling fairways lined with pine trees; large, deep-faced bunkers; and relatively small greens.

In contrast, the East Course is much shorter than the rambling West Course. Designed by Ed Seay, the East Course is renowned for its first tee, positioned on the second story of Grenelefe's conference center, just outside the pro shop. The South Course, designed by Ron Garl in consult with PGA Tour pro Andy Bean, is a fun-to-play layout that, according to Garl, requires the use of every club in your bag. Garl has placed a variety of intriguing hazards throughout the course, such as church-pew bunkers, wandering lagoons, and island greens.

The 6,400-acre Lake Marion is a great spot to drop a line between rounds. Bluegill, crappie, and largemouth bass are the big catches. There are also a full-service marina and facilities for boating and canoeing.

Though it's secluded from big-city environs, Grenelefe's dining offerings are not small-town. The lineup includes the Grene Heron Steak House, where Black Angus beef and fresh seafood are the draw; Camelot Restaurant and Patio, which features alfresco dining and a menu dotted with international favorites; Lancelot's Sports Bar, a sports-themed lounge dominated by a big-screen television; and the Forest Pub, a libation haven overlooking the West Course driving range.

The wide open spaces at Grenelefe.

Things to Know ▼ *Grenelefe Golf & Tennis*

Location ▼	3200 State Road 546, Haines City
	(35 miles west of Orlando)
Phone ▼	(863) 422-7511, (800) 422-5333
Website ▼	www.grenelefe.com
Courses ▼	West Course (18) – Robert Trent Jones Sr.
▼	East Course (18) – Ed Seay
▼	South Course (18) – Ron Garl, Andy Bean
Major Amenities ▼	Four restaurants
▼	Fitness center
▼	Swimming pool
▼	Nature trails
▼	Fishing on Lake Marion
▼	Twenty tennis courts
Business Facilities ▼	55,000 square feet of meeting space
Nearby Attractions ▼	Walt Disney World
▼	Cypress Gardens
▼	Fantasy of Flight
▼	Universal Studios

▲   ▲   ▲

Lake County

THOUGH IT MIGHT BE sacrilegious to some, not everyone who visits central Florida wants to cavort with Mickey, Donald, and Shamu. If you want to avoid the tourist hordes in Orlando, the acknowledged "theme park capital of the world," your best bet is to grab your clubs and head to Lake County, a forty-five-minute drive north of the city and a longtime citrus-producing area.

An engaging mix of rolling hills and lakes (more than 1,000 of them within a 1,200-square-mile border), Lake County is dotted with nature trails, state parks, and quaint small towns like Mount Dora, Clermont, Eustis, and Groveland. The topography in the county, the hilliest in flat Florida, has helped the region evolve into an outdoor sportsman's paradise. Recognized as a professional water skiing capital, Lake County hosts more triathlons than any other community in the world and has the largest glider training school in Florida as well.

Lake County's unique rolling terrain has proven to be an excellent location for golf courses. In recent years, the county has established itself as an important destination for elite college golf tournaments. Highlighting the tourney list is the NCAA Men's Division II Golf Championship in 2002; the NCAA Women's Division I Golf Championship in 2001; the NCAA Division II Golf South Regional in 2000; the annual Boys Florida Junior Invitational Golf Championship; and the Bobbie Clampett NCAA Pro-Am Golf Classic.

With the arrival of several new, wildly undulating layouts, Lake County has quietly become a golf vacation destination that offers golfers affordably priced courses in wide-open, uncongested settings. The greens fees in the region range from $25 to $70 (with summer rates discounted as much as 50%). Accommodations—ranging from a major resort to country inns and small chain hotels—are available at rates lower than those in the Orlando tourist corridor.

If a golfer in the area suggests you "head for the hills," chances are he or she is thinking about the Diamond Players Club in Clermont, which touts itself as "Florida's Mountain Golf Course." First-time visitors to Diamond Players Club can't believe the startling elevation changes before their eyes. The overall elevation changes 190 feet, and the highest point on the course is a remarkable (at least for Florida) 260 feet. The 7,000-yard course has significant elevation changes on sixteen holes, and water comes into play on seven holes.

If you hang around the clubhouse after a round at the Diamond Players Club, you might see a familiar face. The course is owned by several professional athletes, including major league baseball players Todd Stottlemyre of the Arizona Diamondbacks and Andy Benes of the St. Louis Cardinals and 1996 U.S. Open champion Steve Jones. The Diamond Players Club was designed by Terrill LaGree, who gained notoriety as the original project manager/developer of Black Diamond Ranch in Lecanto, Florida.

"Look out for black bear!" is often heard in Lake County, but, rest assured, locals are most likely talking about golf, not wildlife. Black Bear Golf Club in Eustis is another undulating beauty. The P. B. Dye design has large waste bunkers, concave rolling fairways, and speedy, roller-coaster greens. Other courses on a Lake County must-play list include Mission Inn Golf & Tennis Resort in Howey-in-the-Hills, with two, eighteen-hole, tree-laden championship layouts; Country Club of Mount Dora, a classy, wonderfully landscaped residential community course; Deer Island Golf & Lake Club, which overlooks Lake Dora and the village of Mount Dora; and Palisades Country Club, a rolling masterpiece in Clermont.

Things to Know ▼ *Lake County*

Location ▼	45 miles north of downtown Orlando
Phone ▼	(800) 798-1071
Website ▼	www.lakecountyfl.com
Courses ▼	Diamond Players Club (18) – Terrill LaGree
▼	Black Bear Golf Club (18) – P.B. Dye
▼	Mission Inn Golf & Tennis Resort (36) – Charles Clark
▼	Country Club of Mount Dora (18) – Joe Lee
▼	Deer Island Golf & Lake Club (18) – Joe Lee
▼	Palisades Country Club (18) – Joe Lee
Major Amenities ▼	Water skiing
▼	Fishing
▼	Glider flights
Business Facilities ▼	Small group facilities at Mission Inn Golf & Tennis Resort and Lakeside Inn
Nearby Attractions ▼	Citrus Tower
▼	Lakeridge Winery and Vineyards
▼	Renninger's Antique Market
▼	Antique Carriage Museum

▲   ▲   ▲

Mission Inn Golf & Tennis Resort

THESE DAYS, family-owned golf resorts are as much a "dinosaur" as rotary telephones and typewriters. Major corporations and chain hotels dominate ownership, which has standardized many amenities and contributed to a more homogenized industry. At the family-owned Mission Inn Golf & Tennis Resort, thirty miles northwest of Orlando, the environment is one of a well-run resort without an impersonal corporate mindset, however. There isn't a lot of red tape when the resort responds to a guest's request.

A carpetlike green . . . a great caddie. . . . Life is good.

The resort is the brainchild of Nick Beucher, a highly successful Chicago businessman who gambled that golfers would somehow find his golf resort in the gentle rolling hills of Lake County. In 1964, several years before Walt Disney World arrived in Orlando and transformed the area into a tourist mecca, Beucher responded to a Wall Street Journal ad and acquired the Floridian Country Club of Howey-in-the-Hills. He completely restructured the badly neglected eighteen-hole course and debuted the resort's hotel in 1969 as the Mission Inn.

Nestled in the tiny community of Howey-in-the-Hills, the 203-room Mission Inn evokes images of northern California, not central Florida. The Spanish Colonial–style inn sits on a hill and is reminiscent of the colorful and immaculately landscaped missions near San Francisco. The main courtyard is the best place to soak up the ambience. You can lounge in the shade of the walls or stroll around while admiring the painted tile murals from Mexico and South America, the fountain, and the bell tower. Over the years, members of Beucher's family have joined the business and continue to actively operate the resort. The family takes great pride in the Mission Inn, and their positive attitude is reflected at every turn, from the room maids and bellmen to the golf course ranger and head golf professional.

When it's time to head for the golf course, you will essentially be heading for the hills. Mission Inn's El Campeon has the highest elevation changes in Florida. Designed in 1926 by C. E. Clarke of Troon, Scotland, El Campeon, the third oldest course in Florida, has natural hillside contours with tee-to-green elevations up to eighty-five feet. The course is characterized by roller coaster–like fairways lined with oak and cypress trees and two peninsula greens, one island green, and one island tee.

The newer Las Colinas layout, designed in 1992 by former PGA Tour player and NBC broadcaster Gary Koch, is more wide open and forgiving but still a serious challenge. Proper shot placement to open fairways and large, undulating greens is a must to score well. If you aren't tired of the water after playing Las Colinas, where all but two holes have water, head over to nearby Lake Harris, where you can fish for bass and cruise on Mission Inn's forty-nine-passenger, 1930s' river yacht. Other on-site recreation amenities include bicycle and jogging trails, a fitness center, and six tennis courts. Mission Inn's rooms have panoramic views of the golf courses, tennis courts, or lakes.

The treacherous #17 hole on El Campeon separates good golfers from bad.

Things to Know ▼	*Mission Inn Golf & Tennis*
Location ▼	10400 County Road 48, Howey-in-the-Hills (35 miles from downtown Orlando)
Phone ▼	(352) 324-3101, (800) 874-9053
Website ▼	www.missioninnresort.com
Courses ▼	El Campeon (18) – C. E. Clarke
▼	Las Colinas (18) – Gary Koch
Major Amenities ▼	Five restaurants and lounges
▼	Bill Skelley School of Golf (October–May)
▼	Eight tennis courts
▼	Swimming
▼	Jogging and bicycle trails
▼	Antique yacht
▼	Bass and pontoon boat rentals
Business Facilities ▼	30,000 square feet of meeting and banquet space; Teambuilders Outdoor Learning Center
Nearby Attractions ▼	Walt Disney World
▼	Sea World
▼	Universal Studios
▼	Lakeridge Winery and Vineyards
▼	Fiddler's Green Ranch
▼	Renninger's Antique Market

▲   ▲   ▲

Orange County National Golf Center & Lodge

SINCE ITS OPENING four years ago, Orange County National has collected awards at the same pace Tiger Woods has collected major championship trophies. National and local publications have heaped praise on the two eighteen-hole championship courses at the 911-acre complex. Crooked Cat was nominated by Golf Digest as a "Best New Course" in 1999. Its Panther Lake course was tabbed a "Top 10 You Can Play" by Golf Magazine in 1998, and Orange County National was voted "Best Range in America" by Golfer magazine the same year.

Located five miles north of Walt Disney World on a sweeping parcel of former ranch and citrus land, Orange County National, a public/private venture, is a world-class facility that features thirty-six holes of championship golf, a nine-hole executive course, a 33,000-square-foot clubhouse, a 7,000-square-foot pro shop, a forty-two-acre practice range, a fifty-room golf lodge, and the Phil Ritson Golf Institute. Because of its somewhat isolated location away from the tourist area, Orange County National is still a well-kept secret and is normally not crowded. Recently, several housing developments have sprouted nearby, and the complex is booking an increasing number of tee times, but that number is still well below what you would expect at a facility with its impressive amenity lineup.

The two shining stars of that lineup are the long and challenging championship courses that were fashioned by the design team of Isao Aoki, Phil Ritson, and Dave Harmon. Panther Lake incorporates rolling hills and sixty-foot elevation changes as it winds through natural oak hammocks, pine forests, scenic wetlands, and freshwater lakes. Crooked Cat, a wide-open, flowing design, has a distinct "links" flavor with few trees; wide, terraced fairways; large, sloping greens; and native redtop heather grass in the rough, giving it a Scottish feel.

There's absolutely no excuse for not warming up at Orange County National, which has a huge, multidimensional practice facility where golfers can work on every conceivable shot they'll encounter on the course. The practice range might look familiar. It served as the site for the Tiger Woods commercial in which he performed a series of tricks while bouncing a ball off his wedge.

Golf instructor Phil Ritson won't be able to teach you that trick, but he can advise you on every other aspect of a good golf swing. Voted one of "America's Fifty Greatest Teachers" by Golf Magazine, the former South African golf professional and one-time director of golf at Walt Disney World has spent more than five decades teaching juniors, amateurs, and touring professionals. Ritson's on-site institute features a golf studio for videotaping and offers a variety of hourly, half-day, full-day, and multi-day programs.

Since Orange County National is miles away from any tourist distractions, golfers who want to totally embrace the little white ball for a few days usually opt to stay in the fifty-room lodge situated in the center of the complex. Orange County National's stay-and-play packages are among some of the best golf deals in central Florida.

Things to Know ▼ *Orange County National*

Location ▼	16301 Phil Ritson Way, Winter Garden, (6.8 miles north of U.S. 192; 9.5 miles south of Highway 50)
Phone ▼	(407) 656-2626
Website ▼	www.ocngolf.com
Courses ▼	Crooked Cat (18) – Isao Aoki, Phil Ritson, Dave Harmon
▼	Panther Lake (18) – Isao Aoki, Phil Ritson, Dave Harmon
▼	The Tooth (9) – Isao Aoki, Phil Ritson, Dave Harmon
Major Amenities ▼	Fifty-room lodge
▼	Nine-hole executive course
▼	Forty-two-acre practice range
▼	Clubhouse restaurant
▼	Golf institute
Business Facilities ▼	Can accommodate groups up to 250
Nearby Attractions ▼	Walt Disney World
▼	Universal Studios
▼	Sea World

▲   ▲   ▲

Orlando World Center Marriott

THIS GARGANTUAN PROPERTY on 200 acres in Lake Buena Vista looks like a golf resort on steroids. Designed in a contemporary Y shape that gradually steps up to a twenty-eight-story tower, the hotel structure encompasses 2,000 guest rooms that encircle a five-acre activity court—a setting of waterfalls, lagoons, pools, rock-scapes, and exotic landscaping.

The Hawk's Landing Golf Club, which is also open to non-resort guests, wraps around the hotel on three sides. Originally designed by Joe Lee in 1986, the course was given a face-lift by golf architect Bob Cupp in 1999. A great combination of woods, water (affecting fifteen holes), palm trees, rock-scapes, bridges and grass-sloped bunkers make this layout a pleasurable five-mile walk no matter how you play. It's a shotmaker's delight that demands a variety of shots, including low and run-up shots, fades, draws, and an assortment of chip shots.

Because the course surrounds the hotel, almost every room has a view of the tees, greens, or fairways. All of rooms and 111 suites feature light, airy, tropical décor and spacious balconies. For the business traveler/golfer, the rooms provide data ports and high-speed Internet access by STSN.

For those who want to entertain business associates or simply want to follow a round of golf with a celebratory steak dinner, the hotel has two excellent on-site options. For classic, American-grilled steaks, the Hawk's Landing Steakhouse & Grille, a few steps from the course, can accommodate the hungriest of carnivores. For an Oriental flair, Mikado's Japanese Steakhouse features succulently prepared beef and entertaining waiters.

Things to Know ▼ *Orlando World Center Marriott*

Location ▼	One World Center Drive, Orlando (2 miles from Walt Disney World)
Phone ▼	(407) 239-4200, (800) 621-0638
Website ▼	www.marriottresorts.com
Course ▼	Hawk's Landing Golf Club (18) – Joe Lee, Bob Cupp
Major Amenities ▼	Seven restaurants and lounges
▼	Spa
▼	Indoor and outdoor pools
▼	Health club
▼	Twelve tennis courts
▼	Concierge service
▼	Rental car desk
▼	Full business center
▼	Child care services
Business Facilities ▼	214,000 square feet of meeting space
Nearby Attractions ▼	Walt Disney World
▼	Celebration
▼	Downtown Disney shopping and dining complex

▲   ▲   ▲

Walt Disney World

DON'T FRET. At Walt Disney World you don't have to tee off from Space Mountain at the Magic Kingdom, hit drives over the lake at Epcot, or stroll the fairways trading barbs with a fuzzy character named Goofy. Golf at Walt Disney World is a first-class experience and a welcome reprieve from the sometimes grueling days wandering the theme parks.

Like everything else at Walt Disney World—a mega-entertainment complex encompassing 4 separate theme parks, 27 hotels and resorts, and 300 restaurants—the resort's golf offerings are a smorgasbord. Five eighteen-hole courses and one nine-holer are spread among three different complexes.

Here's a cursory glance at Disney's course lineup. (The Magnolia and Palm courses are used as venues in the National Car Rental Classic, a PGA Tour event).

Magnolia: Home to the famous bunker shaped like Mickey Mouse's head, the Magnolia, the longest of the Disney courses, is an engaging mix of 1,500 magnolia trees, 97 bunkers, and 11 water hazards. If you can't make it to the beach, try the Magnolia's 552-yard, par-5 fourth hole, where fourteen bunkers comprising two acres of sand are sprinkled from tee to green.

Palm: Generally regarded as the best Disney layout by golf writers, the Palm is a shotmaker's delight that demands laser-straight drives and approach shots. Dark, deep woods frame most of the sinewy fairways, and water comes into play on nine holes. The Palm's eighteenth hole is almost as terrifying as the Tower of Terror ride at Disney's MGM Studios Theme Park. Since 1983, the PGA Tour has rated the par-4 finishing hole as one of the ten most difficult holes on the entire circuit.

Lake Buena Vista: Nestled inconspicuously behind Downtown

Disney, a massive entertainment/shopping complex, Lake Buena Vista is the easiest of the full-size courses.

Oak Trail: Designed for family play, this walkable, 2,913-yard layout might be where you find Goofy swinging the sticks on his day off.

Eagle Pines: This is presumably Disney's answer to the Carolina sandhills and Pinehurst. A minimalist layout designed by Pete Dye, the course has concave fairways, native grasses, straw and sand waste areas, and topsy-turvy greens.

Osprey Ridge: The massive greens on this Tom Fazio–designed course are almost as large as a typical grocery store parking lot. Take time lining up your putts or you'll have numerous three- and four-putt holes. Constantly changing, the settings on Osprey Ridge range from marshes to dense oak and pine forests to lagoons framed by waste bunkers.

Golfers who choose to stay at any of the seventeen Disney-owned hotels receive some important perks, including early admission to theme parks, discounts, and free transportation throughout the complex. Among the options are the Grand Floridian, the Yacht & Beach Club, the Contemporary Resort, and the Wilderness Lodge and Boardwalk in the expensive category; Coronado Springs and Caribbean Beach in the moderate category; and the All Star Sports Resort, the All-Star Music Resort, and the All-Star Movies Resort in the value category.

The Walt Disney World Swan and Dolphin resort, a huge complex with 2,267 rooms, is centrally located to all of the golf courses and provides an excellent non-Disney-owned hotel option. Whether you stay there or not, Shula's Steak House is a great place to dine after a round. Known for its telephone book–thick steaks, the restaurant is filled with pictures and memorabilia from the 1972 Miami Dolphins' 17-0 perfect season.

Topping the list of must-dine restaurants at Walt Disney World are Artist Point at the Wilderness Lodge, California Grill at the Contemporary Resort, and Citrico's and Victoria and Albert's at the Grand Floridian.

Things to Know ▼ *Walt Disney World*

Location ▼	13 miles from downtown Orlando in Lake Buena Vista
Phone ▼	(407) 939-4653
Website ▼	www.golf.disneyworld.com
Courses ▼	Magnolia (18) – Joe Lee
▼	Palm (18) – Joe Lee
▼	Lake Buena Vista (18) – Joe Lee
▼	Oak Trail (9) – Ron Garl
▼	Eagle Pines (18) – Peye Dye
▼	Osprey Ridge (18) – Tom Fazio
Major Amenities ▼	Four theme parks (Magic Kingdom, Epcot, Disney-MGM Studios, Disney's Animal Kingdom)
▼	Three water adventure parks
▼	Downtown Disney shopping and dining complex
Business Facilities ▼	320,000 square feet of space in five meeting-oriented properties
Nearby Attractions ▼	Universal Studios
▼	Sea World
▼	Gatorland

▲   ▲   ▲

Upper West Coast

1 ● Crystal River

2 ● Brooksville

3 ● Tarpon Springs

4 ● Clearwater
● Tampa
5
● St. Petersburg
6 7

1. Plantation Inn & Golf Resort
2. World Woods Golf Club
3. Westin Innisbrook Resort
4. Belleview Biltmore Resort & Spa
5. Saddlebrook Resort
6. Renaissance Vinoy Resort
7. Tradewinds Island Resorts

Upper 4 West Coast

Belleview Biltmore Resort & Spa

ORIGINALLY BUILT IN 1897 by railroad tycoon Henry B. Plant, the Belleview Biltmore Resort & Spa in Clearwater was one of the nation's first to feature golf as an amenity. Many believe it was the Belleview Biltmore that began the movement of golf from the confines of the country club to the resort hotel. Listed on the National Register of Historic Places, the often-renovated and up-to-date Belleview Biltmore reputedly is the largest occupied wooden structure in the world.

Situated on a high coastal bluff overlooking the Gulf of Mexico and surrounded by pine and oak trees, the large, rambling,

Victorian-style hotel, with its white walls and green gables, offers guests a glimpse of turn-of-the-century opulence. In its early days, the hotel was a favored retreat for celebrities, industrial barons, and international dignitaries, who often traveled in their own railroad cars. Any visitor with even a passing interest in Florida history will thoroughly enjoy the hotel's historical museum, which offers photos, artifacts, and staff uniforms as well as daily historical tours.

Located a mile away from the hotel, the Belleview Biltmore Golf Cub, a classic Donald Ross design built in 1925, has recently received an extensive, multimillion-dollar renovation, including rebuilt greens and tee boxes, new cart paths, and a revamped irrigation and drainage system. A consultant from the Donald Ross Society in Pinehurst, North Carolina, was retained to ensure the course would remain true to Ross's original routing and design.

The Belleview Biltmore's 244 rooms and suites exude Old World flavor. The Queen Anne décor is consistent with the Victorian style of the exterior. In the suites, French doors trimmed in white wood separate sleeping from sitting areas. A European-style spa is a place where you will be exercised, toned, massaged, and refreshed. For a one-of-a-kind dining experience, try the Tiffany Dining Room, named for its priceless, vaulted, stained-glass ceiling.

Things to Know ▼ *Belleview Biltmore Resort & Spa*

Location ▼ 25 Belleview Boulevard, Clearwater
(20 miles west of Tampa International
Airport)

Phone ▼ (727) 442-6171, (800) 237-8947

Website ▼ www.belleviewbiltmore.com

Course ▼ Belleview Biltmore Golf Club (18) –
Donald Ross

Major Amenities ▼ Spa
▼ Four red-clay tennis courts
▼ Large outdoor pool
▼ Children's playground

Business Facilities ▼ 30,000 square feet of meeting space

Nearby Attractions ▼ Clearwater Marine Aquarium
▼ Dolphin Encounter Cruise
▼ Salvador Dali Musium
▼ Florida International Museum
▼ St. Petersburg Museum of History
▼ Tampa Bay Holocaust Memorial
Museum and Education Center

▲　　　▲　　　▲

Plantation Inn & Golf Resort

THE PLANTATION INN & GOLF RESORT in Crystal River is absolutely the best place in the world to see and swim with manatees and play some good, traditional golf on the side. Set along the banks of the Crystal River, the 232-acre resort has its own dive shop and twenty-seven holes of golf.

Crystal River is the "winter home" of the largest concentration of manatees in North America. In this area, the wild manatees allow humans to swim among them, and the Plantation Inn Dive Shop features several programs for guests to see manatees up close and personal. Fed by thirteen freshwater springs at a constant 72°, the Crystal River is a hugely popular freshwater dive site. A full-service marina connected to the dive shop has rental boats, snorkeling and scuba equipment, experienced guides, and complete docking and boat-launching facilities.

For anglers, the Crystal River is one of the state's best fishing areas, with trout, redfish, and bass the most popular catches. A favorite activity is to fish all morning, accompanied by a guide, and eat your catch for lunch on a nearby island.

When you're ready to take a dive into golf, an eighteen-hole championship course, designed by Mark Mahannah, and nine-hole executive layout comprise the Plantation Inn's golf complex. The courses weave around dozens of natural lakes and loblolly pines. For those who don't mind venturing off the property, Plantation Inn has play agreements with ten area courses, including World Woods, with two Tom Fazio courses; Twisted Oaks, a new Karl Litton course; and Southern Woods, a Hale Irwin design.

The Plantation's white-columned inn conjures up images of Southern hospitality—and that's just what you get at this folksy, forty-year-old resort. Accommodations include 126 guest rooms, 12 golf villas, and 5 condominiums.

Things to Know ▼	***Plantation Inn & Golf Resort***
Location ▼	9301 West Fort Island Trail, Crystal River (80 miles north of Tampa)
Phone ▼	(352) 795-4211, (800) 632-6262
Website ▼	www.plantationinn.com
Courses ▼	Plantation Inn & Golf Resort Course (18) – Mark Mahannah
▼	Executive Course (9) – Mark Mahannah
Major Amenities ▼	Large swimming pool
▼	On-site dive shop
▼	Manatee-sighting tours
▼	Fishing charters
▼	Croquet lawn
Business Facilities ▼	8,000 square feet of meeting space
Nearby Attractions ▼	Gulf of Mexico beaches
▼	Cedar Key
▼	Weeki Wachee Springs water park with mermaid shows

▲   ▲   ▲

Renaissance Vinoy Resort

SEVERAL DECADES AGO, before the days of Tiger Woods, cantaloupe-size driver heads, and long putters that look like boat oars, golf was a simpler and more sedate experience. Following a round of golf in the 1930s and '40s, golfers wouldn't troop to the clubhouse for drinks and a big screen television. Rather, they would return to the expansive lobby of their resort hotel for a cool libation or a spot of tea. The ritual provided an opportunity to rec-ollect course heroics and perhaps settle up on wagers.

That tradition isn't dead yet, at least not at the Renaissance Vinoy Resort, the massive, salmon-colored hotel overlooking Tampa Bay. Fully restored in the early 1990s, the legendary, seventy-five-year-old resort in downtown St. Petersburg allows golfers to travel back in time to this bygone era without forgoing modern-day amenities.

A sweeping front veranda—with foliage-framed sitting areas to soak up the Florida sun and enjoy the breeze blowing off Tampa Bay—ushers guests into a luxurious lobby. With its original glazed, quarry tile floor, stenciled cypress beams, Italian marble front desk, and reproductions of 1920s' chandeliers, the lobby evokes the ambience of an elegant Mediterranean resort. Don't miss the hotel's historical tour, on which you'll hear tales about famous guests like Babe Ruth, F. Scott Fitzgerald, and Ernest Hemingway, as well as intricate architectural details. (Tours begin at 10:30 A.M. Wednesday through Saturday.)

While paying homage to its past, the Renaissance Vinoy responds to the demands of today's golfers with an eighteen-hole redesigned golf course, a seventy-slip marina, two swimming pools, five restaurants and lounges, a full-service health club, a salon and day spa, and a twelve-court tennis complex. The 360 tastefully appointed rooms and suites are equipped for twenty-first-century travelers with amenities such as data port capability, two television sets, writing desks, and, of course, coffeemakers and bathrobes.

The Renaissance Vinoy Golf Club, a five-minute drive from the hotel via complimentary limousine service, was restored by golf architect Ron Garl. Based in Lakeland, Florida, Garl has designed more than 130 courses, including the Las Vegas Country Club in Las Vegas, Nevada; Fiddlesticks in Fort Myers, Florida; and Heritage Pointe in Calgary, Canada.

The par-70, 6,267-yard Vinoy layout weaves through a tony residential area on Snell Isle. The meticulously landscaped homes are hardly noticeable, though, as the fairways are framed by mature tree growth and shrubs. Highlights include nine lakes, narrow fairways, pine valleys, and two double greens. Make no mistake—this is not a course that will have low-handicappers shaking in their golf shoes. Simply put, the Renaissance Vinoy Golf Club is the

Mirror, mirror, on the course, please let me hit the green.

quintessential resort course. The toughest holes are seven, eight, and nine, then sixteen, seventeen, and eighteen, so golfers have the opportunity to score well early on the front and back nines. Garl designed the course so golfers can build confidence early, since they'll need it later.

Things to Know ▼	*Renaissance Vinoy Resort*
Location ▼	501 Fifth Avenue NE, St. Petersburg (22 miles south of Tampa International Airport)
Phone ▼	(727) 894-1000
Website ▼	www.renaissancehotels.com
Course ▼	Renaissance Vinoy Golf Club (18) – Ron Garl
Major Amenities ▼	Marina
	▼ Health club
	▼ Salon
	▼ Day spa
	▼ Tennis complex
Business Facilities ▼	27,340 square feet of indoor meeting space
	▼ 22,000 square feet of outdoor function space
Nearby Attractions ▼	Florida International Museum
	▼ Salvador Dali Museum
	▼ BayWalk shopping center
	▼ Major league baseball at Tropicana Field

▲   ▲   ▲

Saddlebrook Resort

IF THERE IS ONE Florida resort that consistently gets it right for golfers, it's Saddlebrook near Tampa. A forerunner of the modern-day golf resort genre, the twenty-one-year old resort, set on 480 acres of palm-, pine- and cypress-dotted terrain, has established itself as one of the state's best golf getaways.

Without a major chain affiliation, Saddlebrook is an anomaly in the golf resort hospitality world. The unpretentious resort is owned and operated by the Dempsey family, originally from Ohio, who respond quickly to requests and suggestions from guests. Through the years, Tom Dempsey and his superb management staff have developed amenity offerings that cater to just about every need and whim of a golf vacationer.

Take a deep breath, because merely reading Saddlebrook's amenity list is enough to make you tired. For golfers, there are two eighteen-hole, Arnold Palmer–designed courses as well as the world headquarters of the Arnold Palmer Golf Academy. Other amenities include a forty-five-court tennis complex and the Harry Hopman Tennis Program; a 270-foot-long SuperPool; a 7,000 square-foot European-style spa featuring thirty-eight body and facial treatments; a sports village with a 3,300-square-foot fitness center, a basketball court, and a sports field; a wellness center focusing on stress reduction and conflict resolution techniques; and S'Kids Club, a program designed for children ages four to twelve.

One of the most appealing aspects of Saddlebrook is that most of its accommodations, its restaurants, and all of its major amenities are never more than a short walk away, thanks to the resort's innovative walking-village concept. No long commutes or vans needed here: simply walk a few steps from your room or suite, and, voilà, you stroll into the pro shop.

Saddlebrook's two courses, the Palmer and the Saddlebrook, are not long, but they are testy because of the undulating terrain, sometimes narrow fairways, and strategically placed bunkers. With fairways that dip like a roller coaster, there are fewer flat lies than you would find at most Florida courses. Towering·cypress and pine trees line the fairways, and accuracy off the tee is imperative. The greens, with their many dips and rolls, resemble Palmer's Bay Hill course in Orlando.

Getting fit for some high-calorie resort dining.

The golf courses surround clusters of 800 rooms and suites. Accommodations at Saddlebrook are comprised of one-, two-, and three-bedroom suites, all of which feature either a patio or balcony overlooking the courses, SuperPool, or nature areas. Suites are complete with kitchens. Saddlebrook recently completed an extensive refurbishment of its guest rooms that included new, colorful furnishings and drapes as well as brass fixtures and a generous use of marble in the bathrooms and kitchens.

Don't leave—I repeat—don't leave Saddlebrook without dining at Dempsey's Steak House. Clubby yet homey and friendly, the restaurant is appointed with rich, dark woods and marble. You'll feel like Mr. Dempsey's personal guest as you gorge on delicacies like New York strip pepper steak and Key West shrimp scampi.

Things to Know ▼	*Saddlebrook Resort*
Location ▼	5700 Saddlebrook Way, Wesley Chapel (30 miles north of Tampa International Airport)
Phone ▼	(813) 973-1111, (800) 729-8383
Website ▼	www.saddlebrookresort.com
Courses ▼	Palmer (18) – Arnold Palmer
▼	Saddlebrook (18) – Arnold Palmer
Major Amenities ▼	Arnold Palmer Golf Academy
▼	Forty-five tennis courts
▼	Harry Hopman Tennis Program
▼	Spa
▼	Sports village
▼	SuperPool
▼	S'Kids Club
▼	Wellness center
Business Facilities ▼	82,000 square feet of meeting space
Nearby Attractions ▼	Busch Gardens
▼	Ybor City
▼	Florida Aquarium

▲　　　▲　　　▲

Tradewinds Island Resorts

FOR THOSE WHO THINK SPLASHING in the surf with sand twinkling between their toes is every bit as important to a Florida getaway experience as sinking a few birdie putts, the Tradewinds Island Resorts on St. Pete Beach should definitely warrant consideration. Set on thirty-five acres of blindingly white sand on the Gulf of Mexico, Tradewinds is an amenity-loaded property with seventeen choices for eating and drinking, nine swimming pools, and an almost-limitless lineup of beachfront recreation. For the "life's a beach" contingent, welcome to Shangri-la.

While Tradewinds lacks an on-site golf course, playing a round or two (or three) is the least of a visitor's worries. Resort guests are afforded exclusive golf privileges at Pasadena Golf & Country Club, a private club with a course designed by John Van Kleek located three miles from the hotel complex. All charges at the course are transferable to room accounts, and individual tee times can be made up to seven days in advance. Other courses the Tradewinds has play agreements with include Bardmoor Country Club in Largo, Mangrove Bay in St. Petersburg, Legacy at Lakewood Ranch in Bradenton, and River Club in Bradenton.

Chances are, you might find it difficult to leave the resort complex, where tropical garden paths and inland waterways enhance a casual environment in which a tropical shirt, bathing suit, and flip-flops are the standard daytime (and, for some, nighttime) attire. Comprised of three separate hotel properties—Island Grand, Sirata Beach Resort, and Sandpiper Hotel—Tradewinds Resorts encompasses 1,124 guest rooms, including 480 suites, penthouses, and hospitality suites.

For beach activities, Tradewinds' list includes beach volleyball, sunset parties, parasailing, jet skiing, and catamaran and paddleboat rides. A great place to celebrate your tan or a good-scoring day on the links is the resort's Palm Court Restaurant. You can dine indoors among the hand-painted murals or on the courtyard patio under the stars. Specializing in gourmet Italian cuisine, the Palm Court's menu is highlighted by two exceptional entrees that are prepared to perfection, the Pan-Seared Salmon au Poivre and the Seafood Risotto.

Things to Know ▼	*Tradewinds Island Resorts*
Location ▼	5500 Gulf Boulevard, St. Pete Beach
Phone ▼	(727) 562-1212, (800) 237-0707
Website ▼	www.tradewindsresort.com
Course ▼	Pasadena Golf & Country Club (18) – John Van Kleek
Major Amenities ▼	Beaches
▼	Nine swimming pools
▼	Seventeen restaurants and lounges
▼	Four tennis courts
▼	Fitness center and salon
▼	Fishing excursions
Business Facilities ▼	50,000 square feet of meeting space
Nearby Attractions ▼	Salvador Dali Museum
▼	Derby Lane greyhound racing
▼	Fort DeSoto Park

▲　　　▲　　　▲

Westin Innisbrook Resort

GENTLEMEN AND LADIES, start your golf carts! One of Florida's best resort courses, Innisbrook's Copperhead is annually rated in everybody's "Top Ten to Play in Florida" list. Site of the PGA Tour's Tampa Bay Classic, the Copperhead actually has more of a North Carolina than a Florida ambience. Its rolling hills and tall pines are reminiscent of the Sandhills of North Carolina.

Novices with shaky swings are best advised to continue driving their carts past Copperhead to another one of Innisbrook's four championship courses. An extremely difficult test, especially from the back tees, which measure more than 7,200 yards, Copperhead has tight fairways heavily lined with trees; seventy-three bunkers; and fast, tricky greens. If you can go eighteen holes without hitting a branch on the tree-laden layout, then it might be time to check the dates for the PGA Tour Qualifying School.

Less heralded but equally rewarding is the Island Course. While many choose it as a "resort" alternative to the daunting Copperhead, it is just as challenging: it's about the same length as Copperhead, has one more bunker, and has water on half the holes. The Island's first six holes are dominated by lateral water hazards that require accuracy on tee shots and approaches.

For a more laid-back resort experience where lower scoring is possible, choose from the Highlands South and North Courses, the latter of which was recently refurbished and lengthened and is in fine shape. Both courses feature lots of waste areas but less water and more room to go astray than Copperhead and Island.

Swing tune-ups and complete overhauls are available at Innisbrook's Troon Golf Institute, which offers a year-round series of comprehensive instruction programs for all skill levels and features a variety of daily clinics, private instruction, and three practice facilities.

Westin Innisbrook is an amenity-happy resort spread over 1,000 pine- and oak-dotted acres. Seven hundred suites in twenty-eight lodges are nestled around the golf courses. Guests may choose from four floor plans, ranging from club suites to the deluxe three-bedroom configuration, each featuring a fully

Alas, someone having fun in a sand bunker.

equipped kitchen and private patio or balcony. Peaceful and shady, the resort is like some beautiful suburb where everyone takes a short daily commute to recreational fun instead of a job. Highlighting the recreation menu are a kid's recreation center with video games and miniature golf, a wildlife preserve with an elevated boardwalk, sixty acres of stocked lakes, and jogging and bicycling trails throughout the vast property. A couple of miles outside the gates is Tarpon Springs, a largely Greek fishing village loaded with shops, restaurants, and local color. The beach is minutes away via the resort's complimentary shuttle service.

You don't need to leave the property, however, for an exceptional dining experience. Topping the list of the resort's five restaurants is DY's Steak House, a fine-dining eatery overlooking the Copperhead golf course that is modeled after Shula's Steak House. A carnivore's Shangri-la, DY's serves Black Angus beef and lobster coupled with a fabulous wine and signature martini list.

Can you name this course?

Things to Know ▼ *Westin Innisbrook Resort*

Location ▼	36750 U.S. Highway 19 North, Palm Harbor (23 miles northeast of Tampa International Airport)
Phone ▼	(727) 942-2000, (800) 456-2000
Website ▼	www.westin-innisbrook.com
Courses ▼	Copperhead (18) – Lawrence Packard
▼	Island Course (18) – Lawrence Packard
▼	Highlands South Course (18) – Lawrence Packard
▼	Highlands North Course (18) – Lawrence Packard
Major Amenities ▼	Five restaurants
▼	Eleven tennis courts
▼	Troon Golf Institute
▼	Six swimming pools, including three-acre superpool
▼	Wildlife preserve
▼	Fitness center
▼	Sixty acres of lakes, jogging and cycling trails
Business Facilities ▼	85,000 square feet of meeting and banquet space
Nearby Attractions ▼	Tarpon Springs Greek fishing village
▼	Busch Gardens
▼	Florida Aquarium

▲   ▲   ▲

World Woods Golf Club

BROOKSVILLE IS A SLEEPY, small town in Florida's mostly rural upper west coast region. It's a place where you half expect a Deputy Barney Fife–type to be sitting in a squad car behind a billboard, munching on a moon pie, sipping a Dr. Pepper, and waiting for city folk speeders. Brooksville is "Old South," not "New Florida." Suffice it to say, you won't find a more unlikely locale for two of the state's best of more than 1,250 golf courses.

Spread out over rolling hills dotted with pines and oaks, World Woods Golf Club is a 2,100-acre complex encompassing two championship, Tom Fazio–designed courses, a nine-hole short course, a twenty-three-acre circular practice range, a three-hole practice course, and a thirty-six-hole putting course. Opened in 1993, World Woods was built by a Japanese billionaire who presumably didn't know much about location but was well versed in championship-style golf. The golf courses and practice facilities have been lauded by every major national and international golf publication.

Should you never get invited to play Pine Valley in New Jersey, one of America's perennially top-rated courses, the next best thing might just be the Pine Barrens Course at World Woods. Sculpted from an expansive pine forest with dramatic changes in elevation, the course has generously wide fairways, many of which are framed by large waste bunkers. Disaster seems to lurk behind nearly every shot, and Fazio never lets you take a break mentally. If you spend too much time thinking about what condiments you want on your burger after the round rather than concentrating on your shot, you'll be in for a long, arduous day.

While Rolling Oaks has a reputation for being easier and more playable than Pine Barrens, it's not easy pickings either.

Despite being built directly adjacent to Pine Barrens, Rolling Oaks is a totally different golf experience. Differences in soil content allow the land to support giant oak trees draped with Spanish moss. Bunkers filled with bleached white sand contrast with lush, carpetlike fairways and many azalea bushes, causing many to compare Rolling Oaks to Augusta National. The back nine at Rolling Oaks is among the toughest in Florida, thanks to holes such as the sixteenth, a 234-yard par-3 from an elevated tee to a green guarded by bunkers and framed by trees. The back nine also features a sinkhole, marked as a hazard.

Unless you're about to miss your tee time, there's absolutely no excuse to miss a practice session before you start your round. The massive range with grass-teeing stations on four sides is, arguably, the best in the world. The arrangement offers a wide variety of target greens, target fairways, and practice bunkers of both native and white sand. Encircling the range are multiple chipping and pitching greens.

Future plans at World Woods call for a third eighteen-hole championship golf course, on-site accommodations, and corporate meeting rooms. Presently, World Woods offers a variety of stay and-play packages with several small chain hotels in the area, including the Best Western Weeki Wachee (352-596-2007), Holiday Inn Brooksville (352-796-9481), and Days Inn Brooksville (352-796-9486). For those who can withstand the humid summer heat, greens fees at World Woods are discounted as much as 60% from May to September.

Things to Know ▼ ***World Woods Golf Club***

Location ▼	17590 Ponce de Leon Boulevard, Brooksville (120 miles north of Tampa)
Phone ▼	(352) 796-5500 (ext. 4 for tee times)
Website ▼	www.worldwoods.com
Courses ▼	Pine Barrens Course (18) – Tom Fazio
▼	Rolling Oaks (18) – Tom Fazio
Major Amenities ▼	Twenty-three-acre practice range
▼	Nine-hole short course
▼	Three practice holes
▼	Thirty-six-hole, two-acre putting course
Business Facilities ▼	Scheduled in next building phase
Nearby Attractions ▼	Weeki Wachee Springs water park with mermaid shows
▼	Homosassa Springs Wildlife Park
▼	Crystal River State Archeological Site

▲   ▲   ▲

Upper East Coast

1. Palm Coast Resort
2. LPGA International
3. The Great Outdoors
4. PGA Village
5. Club Med Sandpiper Village

Upper East Coast 5

Club Med Sandpiper Village

SET ON THE SHORES of the St. Lucie River, Club Med Sandpiper is a sports village/resort where guests can engage in activities that range from playing golf and tennis to swinging on an authentic flying trapeze and water skiing on the river.

For those unfamiliar with the Club Med concept, it was created in 1950, when, during a camping trip with friends, Belgian sportsman Gerard Blitz recognized the need for a unique escape from the hardships of postwar Europe. He placed two small advertisements announcing the first all-inclusive vacation on the island of Majorca. The response was overwhelming, and the Club

Mediterranee was born. Today, Club Med has 120 properties (villages) in forty countries, including three in the U.S. (the other two are in Crested Butte and Copper Mountain, Colorado). In the early years, adventurous young people comprised most of the guests, but recently Club Med's guest list has diversified. To facilitate the right match, Club Med has designated Villages for Adults, Villages for Families, and Villages for Everyone.

At a Club Med village, once you pay for the all-inclusive package, you don't even need to bring along tip money. A Club Med vacation includes round-trip air transportation and ground transfers; accommodations; three meals a day with complimentary

Sun and fun—and they have golf too?

Practice, practice, practice and the birdie putts still won't drop.

beverages (including wine and beer at lunch and dinner); all sports activities, lessons, and equipment; daily activities for children; nightly entertainment; gratuities; and travel insurance. There is a reasonably priced surcharge for weekly golf play and instruction packages.

A designated Village for Families, the recently renovated Club Med Sandpiper is fashioned after an "Old Florida" estate. The entire village is painted in soft gray with accents of blue, turquoise, canary, and mustard. Wooden Adirondack-style tables and chairs, along with giant palm trees and large flowering plants, are scattered throughout the village square. There are two restaurants, one featuring various buffets, the other a riverside dining room for adults only. Each of the 338-rooms has cable television and a mini-fridge.

Golf is an integral part of the sports lineup at Sandpiper. There are two on-site championship courses designed by Mark Mahanna; a nine-hole, par-3 course for beginners; practice facilities; and the Golf Academy at Club Med Sandpiper. For linksters who want to pursue other play possibilities, the Ballantrae Golf Club, a Jack Nicklaus Signature course, is located adjacent to the village, and the PGA Golf Club at the Reserve, with two Tom Fazio–designed layouts, is a twenty-minute drive away.

While you're swinging away on the course, rest assured that your children will be living it up in another corner of the village. Among the kids' activities are circus workshops with trapeze, trampoline, and juggling classes; water-skiing lessons on the St. Lucie River; scuba diving in the pool with tiny tanks and fins (ages four and up); beach volleyball; in-line skating lessons; and boat trips.

Things to Know ▼	*Club Med Sandpiper Village*
Location ▼	3500 Southeast Morningside Boulevard, Port St. Lucie (45 miles north of West Palm Beach)
Phone ▼	(561) 398-5100, (800) CLUBMED
Website ▼	www.clubmed.com
Courses ▼	Sinners Course (18) – Mark Mahannah
▼	Club Med Sandpiper Resort Course (18) – Mark Mahannah
Major Amenities ▼	Four swimming pools
▼	Nineteen tennis courts
▼	Two restaurants
▼	Fitness room
▼	Big Top Circus tent with flying trapeze
▼	In-line skating school
▼	ATP Tour tennis camp
Business Facilities ▼	700-person theater; 200-person ballroom
Nearby Attractions ▼	Palm Beach shopping
▼	New York Mets spring training in Port St. Lucie
▼	Los Angeles Dodgers spring training in Vero Beach

▲   ▲   ▲

The Great Outdoors

PULL UP IN YOUR OVERSIZE RV at your typical golf resort and most likely you'll be met with a stare, perhaps a smirk, and an admonishment to park out back somewhere. But if you pull up at the Great Outdoors Resort, you'll be treated like royalty.

The gated community is a resort/residential golf-oriented property where the RV is king. Set on a beautiful parcel of land with lakes, sabal palms, oaks, and pines, the Great Outdoors has double-wide, paved, lighted streets and wide turnouts convenient-ly placed throughout the park. Every RV site is at a 60° angle for easy parking. All RV sites have level, concrete pads and a patio, 30/50-amp electricity, and hookups for cable TV, water, and sewer. Some sites are along the golf course, others are by the lakes, and still others back up to native foliage. No RV sites are back-to-back and there are no pull-through sites.

The brainchild of Jack Eckerd, founder of the billion-dollar Eckerd Drug empire, the Great Outdoors is an innovative project offer-ing RV sites for purchase as well daily, weekly, and monthly hookups. In addition, there are park homes (small, modular-type homes with no more than 600 square feet of living space) available for rent.

Besides the RV lifestyle, what brings everyone together at the Great Outdoors is the high-quality, Ron Garl–designed golf course. Garl worked diligently to preserve the natural contour of the land, and playing the course is much like walking through a wildlife refuge. Egrets and other birds always seem to be craning their necks to watch your shot. You also might catch a glimpse of a deer or rabbit. The course is appointed with paved cart paths, wooden bridges that span wetlands, and white-sand bunkers. Water? It comes into play on all but three holes.

Course amenities are equal to what you might find at any top-notch golf resort. The complex has a lighted aqua range, a fifteen-hole putting green, a chipping area with sand bunker, a fully outfitted pro shop, and teaching professionals on duty.

Suffice it to say, you don't really have to rough it at the Great Outdoors, where other amenities include four tennis courts, two heated swimming pools, two hot tubs, a recreation hall with dance floor, a nature center/library, and a post office. For anglers, the property is dotted with twenty-two stocked fishing lakes where largemouth bass, crappie, and brim are the most popular catches.

Things to Know ▼	*The Great Outdoors*
Location ▼	135 Plantation Drive, Titusville (on S.R. 50, 1/2 mile west of I-95 from Exit 79)
Phone ▼	(800) 621-2267
Website ▼	www.tgoresort.com
Courses ▼	Great Outdoors Resort Course (18) – Ron Garl
Major Amenities ▼	Golf clubhouse
	▼ Restaurant and lounge
	▼ General store and deli
	▼ Nature center and walking trails
	▼ Crafts center
	▼ Non-denominational church
	▼ Post office
	▼ Two swimming pools
	▼ Four tennis courts
Business Facilities ▼	None available
Nearby Attractions ▼	Astronaut Hall of Fame
	▼ Kennedy Space Center
	▼ Merritt Island Wildlife Refuge

▲   ▲   ▲

LPGA International

NOT ALL GOLF COURSES are designed with women in mind. Women's tees on some layouts are almost an afterthought, creating ill-conceived holes that require more strength than strategy. Often women are forced to hit different clubs than men for their second and approach shots. At the LPGA International in Daytona Beach, this problem has been addressed on both of its championship courses, which have five sets of tees. The strategically positioned tee areas encourage each player in a foursome to play the same club for each shot on a hole.

Designed by Rees Jones, the Champions Course is a long, wide-open test that measures 7,088 yards from the back tees. Opened in 1994, the Champions played host for five years to the Titleholders Presented by Mercury Tournament, an LPGA event, and serves as the annual site for the LPGA Tour's Final Qualifying School. A links-style design, the course has innovative mounding and sculpting, marsh areas, nature preserves, and numerous lakes and bunkers.

Built in 1998, the newer Legends Course is an Arthur Hills design with tight, well-bunkered greens, rolling fairways, and water on more than half of the holes. Beautiful magnolias and tall pines line fairways, which have generous landing areas. A nice touch is the "Tip FORE the Week" feature provided on the Prolink GPS computerized yardage system that is on every golf cart. The color monitor shows the exact yardage to the pin and green and provides a tip for playing each hole from an LPGA Tour member.

Golf widows or widowers, or anyone, for that matter, who wants to learn the game, should strongly consider the LPGA Teaching Academy, a world-class facility with three championship practice holes, five putting greens and chipping greens, practice bunkers, and a 360-yard, double-ended driving range. The academy, golf courses, and LPGA Headquarters are located in the LPGA International residential community, a master-planned development dominated by classy stucco homes and impressive landscaping. Nearby lodging options include the Holiday Inn Indigo Lakes and La Quinta Inn Daytona Beach.

Things to Know ▼	*LPGA International*
Location ▼	1000 Champions Drive, Daytona Beach (5 miles north of Daytona Beach)
Phone ▼	(904) 274-LPGA
Website ▼	www.lpga.com
Courses ▼	Champions Course (18) – Rees Jones
▼	Legends Course (18) – Arthur Hills
Major Amenities ▼	Courses designed for women's play
▼	LPGA Golf Academy
Business Facilities ▼	None available
Nearby Attractions ▼	Daytona International Speedway
▼	Daytona USA interactive motor sports attraction
▼	Adventure Landing water theme park
▼	23 miles of beaches at Daytona Beach

▲   ▲   ▲

Palm Coast Resort

SOME OVERZEALOUS GOLF WRITERS have already dubbed Jack Nicklaus's two-year-old Ocean Hammock Golf Club course at Palm Coast as the "East Coast answer to Pebble Beach." Most impartial golf experts agree it's too early to make that claim, yet few dispute that Ocean Hammock is one of the most electrifying courses to be built in Florida in the past few years.

Ocean Hammock has six holes overlooking the Atlantic Ocean, and the drama reaches a crescendo at the end of each nine. Both the ninth and eighteenth holes front sandy beach and crashing surf, presenting a stunning combination of challenge and beauty. Several other holes offer views of the ocean, and the inland holes have natural dunes, rolling ravines, thick stands of pine and oak, and numerous freshwater hazards. The design is quintessentially Nicklaus, with daunting par-4s to close each nine, a series of demanding par-5s, and tricky greens on almost every hole.

Ocean Hammock is the fifth championship golf course at Palm Coast. If you stay for a full, five-day "work" week, you'll have a different course to play each day. Here's the rest of the lineup.

Cypress Knoll: A Gary Player design that conforms to the boundaries of native wetlands and natural lakes, with sinewy fairways that demand accurate tee shots.

Palm Harbor: Carved from stands of tall palms and pines, this Bill Amick design has thirteen dogleg holes.

Pine Lakes: An Arnold Palmer/Ed Seay design that has tight fairways with rolling mounds along the sides and large, well-guarded greens.

Matanzas Woods: A second Palmer/Seay design with an abundance of rolling fairways and water, large greens, and different looks on every hole.

Palm Coast is a sweeping, twenty-five-year-old, 42,000-acre, master-planned residential/resort community between St. Augustine and Daytona Beach. Boating enthusiasts will find Palm Coast Resort an ideal starting point for cruise or fishing expeditions on the Atlantic Ocean or Intracoastal Waterway. Overlooking the Intracoastal, the 154-room hotel is adjacent to an eighty-four-slip marina featuring boat rentals and a ship's store. A newly renovated lobby, appointed in a nautical theme with rich navy, burgundy and gold furnishings, greets visitors. Guest rooms are spacious, with oversize baths, and every room and suite has a view of the Intracoastal or marina.

For those seeking a libation celebration with a heavy dose of fishing, boating, and golf stories, try Henry's Harbourside Bar at the resort, a favorite with locals. A more sedate and romantic ambience is available at Flagler's, the resort's fine-dining restaurant that specializes in seafood, steaks, and regional specialties.

When was the last time you played in an Ocean?

Things to Know ▼ ***Palm Coast Resort***

Location ▼	300 Clubhouse Drive, Palm Coast (60 miles south of Jacksonville just off I-95)
Phone ▼	(904) 445-3000, (800) 654-6538
Website ▼	www.palmcoastresort.com
Courses ▼	Ocean Hammock (18) – Jack Nicklaus
▼	Cypress Knoll (18) – Gary Player
▼	Palm Harbor (18) – Bill Amick
▼	Pine Lakes (18) – Arnold Palmer, Ed Seay
▼	Matanzas Woods (18) – Arnold Palmer, Ed Seay
Major Amenities ▼	Two miles of private seashore
▼	Four swimming pools
▼	Eighteen-court tennis center with hard, clay, and grass courts
▼	Eighty-four-slip marina
▼	Hiking and biking trails
Business Facilities ▼	11,000 square feet of meeting space
Nearby Attractions ▼	World Golf Village
▼	St. Augustine
▼	Daytona International Speedway

▲   ▲   ▲

PGA Village

TYPICALLY WHEN YOU SEE the names Tom Fazio and Pete Dye listed as course designers, you can safely assume you won't get much change back from the hundred-dollar bill you hand over at the pro shop to cover greens fees. Fazio and Dye are universally recognized as two of the best course designers in the modern era, each with numerous layouts in everybody's Top 100 to Play list. At the PGA Village, a 3,000-acre gated complex in Port St. Lucie, the dynamic duo has designed fifty-four holes (thirty-six by Fazio and eighteen by Dye). And the greens fees are surprisingly affordable.

How would you like to drive a Fazio or Dye for $26? It's true. To encourage play, promote the game, and introduce players to world-class golf, the PGA of America has set greens fees as low as $26 certain times of the year. Courses of this quality in Florida typically garner fees between $75 and $100.

Let's peruse the golf menu, shall we? First, the Fazio courses. The South Course is pure Florida, with sloped greens and tricky doglegs set against a backdrop of wetlands, palm trees, and palmettos. Decidedly different is the North Course, which has a Carolina feel—rolling hills and towering pine trees. The Pete Dye Course is built in the tradition of an old Scottish course, with the outward nine leading you away from the clubhouse. Among the distinguishing characteristics of the course are a 100-acre wetland, pine-straw roughs, and grass-based bunkers.

Owned and operated by the PGA of America, the thirty-five-acre PGA Learning Center is arguably the most comprehensive teaching facility in the world. Under the guidance of Director of Instruction Rick Martino, the PGA's 1997 Teacher of the Year and a Master PGA Professional, the complex is equipped to help everyone from banana ball–hitting novices to young phenoms prepping for a professional career.

The PGA Learning Center's teaching amphitheater, reserved specifically for student instruction, features videotaping and swing analysis, a private practice tee area, and three practice holes, each with water hazards and two-tiered greens. In addition, there are a 15,000-square-foot putting green, over one hundred individual practice tees, a twenty-five-station chipping area, and a green-side bunker area with designs inspired from actual courses around the world and five different types of sand.

Keeping with the high-quality theme, the PGA Village has first-class accommodations. Sheraton's PGA Vacation Resort offers one- and two-bedroom villas and one-bedroom efficiencies with screened porches. Luxurious, single-family homes are also available for rent. All guest accommodations feature full kitchens, laundry facilities, and pool access.

Things to Know ▼ *PGA Village*

Location ▼	9700 Reserve Boulevard, Port St. Lucie (40 miles north of Palm Beach)
Phone ▼	(561) 466-6766, (877) 519-6766
Website ▼	pgavillage.com
Courses ▼	South Course (18) – Tom Fazio
▼	North Course (18) – Tom Fazio
▼	Pete Dye Course (18) – Pete Dye
Major Amenities ▼	Thirty-five-acre PGA Learning Center
▼	Swimming
▼	Tennis
Business Facilities ▼	None available
Nearby Attractions ▼	New York Mets spring training in Port St. Lucie
▼	Shopping at Rodeo Drive in Palm Beach
▼	Jupiter Inlet Lighthouse

▲   ▲   ▲

Space Coast

TEN . . . NINE . . . EIGHT . . . SEVEN . . . SIX . . . Hopefully you recognize those numbers as the familiar countdown at Cape Canaveral, home of the nation's space program, and not the digits typically appearing on your scorecard. Situated thirty-five miles east of Orlando, the Space Coast is a seventy-two-mile stretch of beach on the Atlantic Ocean encompassing Cape Canaveral and the Kennedy Space Center as well as beach towns like Cocoa Beach, Melbourne, and Indialantic. Port Canaveral, a bustling, cruise ship port that is home to five cruise lines including the Disney Cruise Line, is also located on Florida's Space Coast.

For golfers, the Space Coast has a lineup of twenty-five, affordably priced, public-access layouts and numerous, moderately priced lodging possibilities. The headliner course in the region is Baytree National Golf Links, a Gary Player Signature design that has been voted Brevard County's best for six years in a row by the readers of Florida Today newspaper. Spanning over 180 acres, with miles of lagoons and spectacular wildlife, Baytree is a joy to play whether you're a struggling novice with a scorecard perpetually dotted with bogeys or a low-handicapper with professional aspirations. There are five different tee markers on every hole, which create a playable layout for all skill levels.

Other courses of note include Habitat at Valkaria, a wonderful combination of natural habitats, imaginative topographic features, and rolling fairways that is one of Florida's best public course values; Majors Golf Club, an Arnold Palmer Signature course with generous fairway landing areas and smallish greens; Viera East Golf Club, where designer Joe Lee has routed the course through marsh wetlands and lakes that are an integral part of every hole; and Turtle Creek Golf Club, a well-maintained layout with heavily wooded fairways and winding creeks.

While there aren't any expansive golf resorts on the Space Coast, the region has a more-than-adequate lineup of beachside chain hotels (Hampton Inn, Courtyard by Marriott, Best Western, Holiday Inn, etc.) that offer golf packages through a company called Tee Times USA (888-465-3356, www.teetimesusa.com).

When you tire of launching golf balls, rest assured that no sojourn to the area is complete without a visit to the area's space launch–oriented attractions. The Kennedy Space Center Visitor Complex has exhibits and memorabilia dating from Alan Shepherd to the latest space shuttle mission. Some of the don't-miss highlights are tours of NASA's space shuttle facilities; the vehicle assembly building, one of the largest buildings in the world; the IMAX 3-D space movie; and the Apollo/Saturn V Center. The nearby Astronaut Hall of Fame has the largest collection of astronaut artifacts in the world as well as a Mission on Mars rover ride, a flight simulator, and a replica cockpit of a Mercury spacecraft. If you want to plan a trip around a space shuttle launch or one of the unmanned rockets launched throughout the year, the best number to call is NASA at (321) 867-4636. On the Internet, check www.patrick.af.mil or www.space.com/missionlaunches for updates.

Whew, finally made it over the water.

Things to Know ▼ *Space Coast*

Location ▼	Space Coast Office of Tourism, 8810 Astronaut Boulevard, Cape Canaveral (35 miles east of Orlando)
Phone ▼	(800) 872-1969 (Space Coast Office of Tourism)
Website ▼	www.space-coast.com
Courses ▼	Baytree National Golf Links (18) – Gary Player
▼	Habitat at Valkaria (18) – Chuck Ankrom
▼	Majors Golf Club (18) – Arnold Palmer
▼	Viera East Golf Club (18) – Joe Lee
▼	Turtle Creek Golf Club (18) – unknown
Major Amenities ▼	Seventy-two miles of beaches
▼	Major cruise port
▼	Space-oriented attractions
▼	Marinas for charter deep-sea fishing
Business Facilities ▼	Meeting space for small groups at a variety of national chain hotels
Nearby Attractions ▼	Kennedy Space Center Visitor Complex
▼	Astronaut Hall of Fame
▼	Port Canaveral

▲   ▲   ▲

Southeast

1 Palm Beach Gardens

2 West Palm Beach

3 Palm Beach

4 Boca Raton

5 Fort Lauderdale

6 Hollywood

Miami Lakes 7 Aventura

8

9 Miami

10 Coral Gables

1. PGA National Resort & Spa
2. Palm Beach Polo & Country Club
3. The Breakers
4. Boca Raton Resort & Club
5. TPC at Heron Bay
6. Westin Diplomat Resort & Spa
7. Turnberry Isle Resort and Club
8. Don Shula's Hotel & Golf Club
9. Doral Golf Resort & Spa
10. The Biltmore Hotel

6

Southeast

The Biltmore Hotel

THE '20S WERE ROARING, and the rich and famous played golf by day and danced the night away when the Biltmore Hotel in Coral Gables debuted in 1926. Built by George E. Merrick, who developed Coral Gables and founded the University of Miami, the Biltmore was the unquestioned hub for social activity in the Miami area. Through the early years—whether it was a lavish fashion show, a gala ball, a golf tournament, or an aquatic show at its gigantic swimming pool—the Biltmore, an official National Historical Landmark, was a celebrity magnet that attracted the likes of the Duke and Duchess of Windsor, Judy Garland, Ginger Rogers, Al Capone, and assorted Roosevelts and Vanderbilts.

One of the important keys to the Biltmore Hotel's success, then and now, is its residential location in the affluent Miami suburb of Coral Gables. Merrick instituted strict building codes, and the town is routed with broad, planted boulevards lined with stately, Mediterranean-style homes. A focal point of Coral Gables, the Spanish-style hotel is easily identified from a distance by its majestic, 300-foot, copper-clad tower, inspired by the Giralda bell tower in Seville. The exquisite craftsmanship and detail found throughout the Biltmore is reminiscent of an Old World, luxury hotel. Guests enter through a spacious, ornate lobby with forty-five-foot-high ceilings. The opulence continues in the 280 fully updated and refurbished guest rooms and suites, which have rich tapestries, elegant upholstered furniture, and European feather beds. On the seventh floor, the exclusive Cellar Club offers deluxe amenities, wine tastings, and nightly hors d'oeuvres.

Directly behind the hotel sits the eighteen-hole, par-71 golf course designed by legendary architect Donald Ross in 1925. In its early years, the course was a mandatory stop for big-name players like 1958 U.S. Open Champion Tommy Bolt, who still visits regularly, and Sam Snead. With its lush, well-manicured, rolling layout, the course captures the essence of Ross designs, with strategically placed bunkers and challenging greens that have subtle dips and contours.

Presumably, the second most popular recreational activity at the Biltmore is swimming in the 22,000-square-foot pool, the largest hotel pool in the continental U.S. In the early 1930s, the pool hosted glamorous aquatic shows featuring celebrities such as Esther Williams and Johnny "Tarzan" Weissmuller. Families would attend the shows, then dress up and go dancing afterwards on the hotel's grand terrace to the sounds of Big Band music.

Overlooking the pool is the hotel's French restaurant, La Palme d'Or, a stunning, 110-seat dining room with enormous crystal chandeliers, colorful frescoes, and expensive Spanish chairs. The restaurant features an evolving menu and a different guest chef from France each month. A favorite spot for cigar-loving golfers is The Courtyard, which features a "Cigars Under the Stars" program on Friday nights that offers alfresco dining, an authentic cigar roller, premium cigars, and cigars paired with different dishes. The Biltmore's Sunday brunch, annually rated by local publications as the best in the Miami area, is a must-attend event with numerous food stations dotting the hotel's huge wraparound terrace and entertainment by a Spanish guitarist and harpist.

Things to Know ▼ *The Biltmore Hotel*

Location ▼	1200 Anastasia Avenue, Coral Gables
Phone ▼	(800) 727-1926, (305) 445-1926
Website ▼	www.biltmorehotel.com
Courses ▼	Biltmore Golf Club (18) – Donald Ross
Major Amenities ▼	Four restaurants
▼	15,000-square-foot fitness center and spa
▼	Ten tennis courts
▼	Huge swimming pool
Business Facilities ▼	48,000 square feet of meeting space
Nearby Attractions ▼	Miami Seaquarium
▼	Vizcaya Museum and Gardens
▼	Venetian Pool
▼	Bayside Marketplace shopping in downtown Miam
▼	CocoWalk shopping complex in Coconut Grove

▲   ▲   ▲

Boca Raton Resort & Club

WHEN LEGENDARY, ECCENTRIC ARCHITECT Addison Mizner acquired a large parcel of Boca Raton property in the early 1920s, he made a vow to create "the greatest resort in the world," a spectacular combination of Venice and Heaven, Florence and Toledo, with a little Greco-Roman glory and opulence thrown in for good measure.

The Cloister, the original hotel structure, a flamingo pink, Spanish castle–like building, still greets guests when they enter the gated resort grounds. Innovative and eclectic, the Cloister is accented with lavish formal gardens and courtyards and furnished with rare antiques from old churches and universities in Spain and Central America. The "Boca," as regulars affectionately call it, has one of America's truly great hotel lobbies, an expansive hall with French terra-cotta floors dotted with handmade rugs from India, priceless antiques, massive floral arrangements, and plush, pillow-happy couches for patrons to sit and watch the colorful passing parade of guests and visitors.

A monument to the luxury lifestyle of early Florida, well before theme parks and chain restaurants, the Boca preserves its past but stays committed to the future. The resort annually spends more than $10 million to refurbish guest rooms and update and add new amenities. In celebration of its seventy-fifth anniversary in 2001, the resort debuted the waterfront Marina Wing Hotel, with 121 luxury rooms and meeting space, a new Tuscan-inspired gourmet restaurant called Lucca, and the 50,000-square-foot Cloister Spa.

In 1998, the Boca spent millions of dollars to update its Resort Course, which has a storied legacy all its own. Opened in

1926, the Resort Course had only two pros for its first forty-four years of operation, Tommy Armour (1926–1955) and Sam Snead (1956–1970). Every celebrity who ever swung a golf club—from Gerald Ford and George Bush to Frank Sinatra and Sylvester Stallone—has played the Resort Course.

The Resort Course underwent many significant changes under the design direction of architect Gene Bates, including the addition of extensive water features and a variety of elevation changes. Water comes into play throughout most of the course, with lakes increased from three acres to twelve. The new, improved Resort Course has a central elevation of more than thirty feet and an island green completing the course on the eighteenth hole. To maintain the tradition of the course, many of the tees and bunkers were fashioned to their original design.

A second course available to resort guests, the Country Club Course, a Joe Lee design located six miles northwest of the hotel, offers a posh, country-club atmosphere. Boca guests are also accorded play privileges at Grande Oaks, a course recently redesigned by Raymond Floyd, in west Ft. Lauderdale. Additionally, whether you're a hacker just starting to play the game or you're tuning up for a run at professional golf, the Boca has some of the best golf instruction in the world available to its resort guests with the Nicklaus/Flick Golf Academy and the Dave Pelz Short Game School.

Guests can choose from six types of lodging at the 356-acre Boca Raton Resort & Club. The Cloister has 338 rooms in the original Mediterranean building, and the Palm Court Club has 49 concierge-level rooms and suites in an exclusive section of the Cloister. The Tower features 153 rooms, 76 junior suites, and 13 suites in a contemporary, twenty-seven-story high-rise with ocean views. The Boca Beach Club has 205 rooms and 9 suites in a low-rise building on a half mile of private Atlantic Ocean beachfront.

The Golf Villas has 120 rooms and suites, some with kitchens, set apart from the main hotel with direct access to the golf course. Finally, there's the previously mentioned Marina Wing Hotel.

Things to Know ▼	*Boca Raton Resort & Club*
Location ▼	501 East Camino Real, Boca Raton (28 miles from Palm Beach International Airport)
Phone ▼	(800) 327-0101, (561) 447-3000
Website ▼	www.bocaresort.com
Courses ▼	Resort Course (18) – William Flynn, Robert Trent Jones Sr., Gene Bates
▼	Country Club Course (18) – Joe Lee
Major Amenities ▼	Eight restaurants and lounges
▼	Five swimming pools
▼	Three fully equipped fitness centers
▼	Spa
▼	Thirty tennis courts
▼	Twenty-five-slip marina
▼	Half-mile private beach
Business Facilities ▼	80,000-square-foot Mizner Center
Nearby Attractions ▼	Hotel historical tour
▼	Mizner Park Shopping Center
▼	Worth Avenue shopping district in Palm Beach
▼	Polo at the Royal Palm Polo Sport Club from January through April

---

▲   ▲   ▲

The Breakers

AT FIRST GLANCE, the Breakers in Palm Beach, a massive, seven-story hotel inspired by the famous Villa Medici in Florence, looks like a pretentious monument to opulence that might be very accommodating to "Joseph Golfer" but not necessarily "Joe Golfer." Fortunately, the Breakers, a venerable favorite of the champagne-and-caviar set, has become less standoffish and more affordable over the years, giving more people the opportunity to enjoy its elegant, sophisticated, resort lifestyle.

Built in the late 1800s by Standard Oil icon Henry Morrison Flagler and listed on the National Register of Historic Places, the Breakers is set on 140 acres of some of the most expensive beachfront property in the world. If you don't have the time or inclination to travel to Europe for a golf getaway, the Breakers is overflowing with European ambience. The Florentine fountain in front of the Italian Renaissance–style hotel is similar to the one in Boboli Gardens in Florence. The main lobby was inspired by the Great Hall of the Palazzo Carega in Genoa.

In addition to its new spa and beach club, one of the most welcomed enhancements at the Breakers has been the recent refurbishment of its Ocean Course, which was originally laid out in 1897 and is considered Florida's oldest eighteen-hole course. The golf course revitalization has transformed the layout from a relatively easy, flat track into a magnificent, mounded, modern-day resort course. Brian Silva, a Boston-based golf architect who specializes in high-profile restoration projects, reshaped, recontoured, and regrassed the entire course. He elevated putting surfaces and flanked them with deeply recessed vintage bunkers and close-cut "green surrounds" that make possible a variety of recovery shots. He also added eighty-eight new and rebuilt bunkers, new cart paths, and state-of-the-art turf grass from tee to green.

The resort's second course, the Breakers West, a fifteen-minute drive from the hotel via complimentary transportation, is a flat layout in a residential community that was originally designed by Willard Byrd in 1968 and later updated by Joe Lee.

Did anyone in the hotel see my birdie putt?

During the summer months, the Breakers drops its rates and offers competitively priced golf packages. Golfers with families will find the Breakers very accommodating in the new millennium as well. As part of its recent $100-million renovation program, a majority of the resort's soundproof rooms were connected, allowing families the opportunity to reserve up to five adjoining guest rooms. Any doubt about the Breakers' new commitment to families is dispelled when kids and parents discover the resort provides Barney, Lion King, and Aladdin sleeping bags at no additional charge. Enhancing the vacation experience for families is the resort's superb Coconut Crew Camp children's program, a series of supervised activities for kids aged three to twelve.

Amid the pampering that parents and kids receive at the Breakers—the hotel has a 1,700-member staff, for a guest-to-staff ratio rivaling that of a cruise ship—guests can engage in a long list of dining and recreational pursuits. Savoring a thick, juicy steak at the Breakers' traditional Flagler Steakhouse; luxuriating in a massage performed outdoors along the ocean in a private tent; and playing a leisurely game of croquet are just a few of the many ways to relax and enjoy your time away from golf.

Things to Know ▼ *The Breakers*

Location ▼	One South County Road, Palm Beach (7 miles from Palm Beach International Airport)
Phone ▼	(888) 273-2537, (561) 655-6611
Website ▼	www.thebreakers.com
Courses ▼	Ocean Course (18) – Brian Silva
▼	Breakers West (18) – Willard Byrd, Joe Lee
Major Amenities ▼	Nine restaurants and lounges
▼	Spa
▼	Beach club and fitness center
▼	Tennis complex
▼	Children's program
▼	Historical tours
▼	Croquet
▼	Jogging trail
▼	On-site boutique shopping
Business Facilities ▼	60,000 square feet of meeting space
Nearby Attractions ▼	Worth Avenue shopping district in Palm Beach
▼	Deep-sea fishing
▼	Scuba diving

▲   ▲   ▲

Westin Diplomat Resort & Spa

IN THE 1960s AND '70s, the Westin Diplomat represented south Florida's answer to the glitzy, mega-hotels that were making Las Vegas famous. The original Diplomat was a hybrid version, without the casinos of the Desert Inn and Tropicana. Big-name performers like Frank Sinatra and Jackie Gleason were regulars on the Diplomat golf course, giving the resort a heavy dose of credibility and high visibility. The word quickly spread that if you wanted to play golf amid swaying palms and Florida breezes, drink a martini or two at the clubhouse, and then luxuriate in a Vegas-style hotel room, the Diplomat was the place to do it.

In the 1990s, however, the Diplomat's only resemblance to the "Rat Pack" was authentic rodents. The resort had not changed with the times, and rigor mortis had set in. The hotel was outdated and unappealing to baby boomers who wanted spas and kids' programs, not high-balls and Big Band entertainment. So in 1998 the original Diplomat was imploded, and $600 million was spent to create the Westin Diplomat Resort & Spa near Ft. Lauderdale.

Florida-based golf architect Joe Lee modernized the golf course, which was reopened in March 2000. Lee's 6,700-yard course is a quintessential south Florida golf experience. The course is peppered with lush foliage, including hundreds of fifty-year-old coconut palms and Cuban laurel, gumbo limbo, bougainvillea, and banyan trees. Surrounding lakes on the course total more than eight acres and affect play on thirteen holes. In addition to prevailing southeast crosswinds from the Intracoastal Waterway and Atlantic Ocean, finely crushed coquina rock in waste bunkers and 16-foot mounds provide obstacles on many holes.

To be sure, the Westin Diplomat loves palm trees on and

off the course. Upon entering the sixty-foot-high lobby/atrium of the main hotel, guests stroll through a corridor of forty-eight palm trees in four rows of twelve. The guest rooms and suites in this thirty-nine-story, 1,000-room hotel offer updated Art Deco style accented by light-colored stone and marble coupled with dark woods.

For those who want accommodations on the golf course rather than on the beach, the Northern Italian villa–style clubhouse has sixty guest rooms, all featuring verandas and golf-course views. Even non-golfing spouses will like the location. Huh? Yes, the country club is connected by a skywalk to the resort's 30,000-

The Westin Diplomat's clubhouse is a peaceful haven after a great—or even less-than-great—round of golf.

square-foot, European-style spa, where seventeen treatment rooms, a full-service salon, saunas and steam rooms, whirlpools, outdoor patios, and programs in fitness, nutrition, face and body care, and lifestyle management await.

The Westin Diplomat's signature restaurant is Marty's, where a masculine, New England–style, gentlemen's club ambience is enhanced with dark woods, leather accents, and nautically themed art. You half expect Ol' Blue Eyes himself to be sitting in a corner booth with his pals. After dinner, the action cranks up at the resort's Celebrity Lounge, which overlooks the ocean and features a center stage and dance floor. Other amenities include ten clay tennis courts and on-site tennis pro, a 240-foot lagoon pool with a see-through bottom and two waterfalls, a marina and private beach, and cabanas.

Things to Know ▼	*Westin Diplomat Resort & Spa*
Location ▼	501 Diplomat Parkway, Hallandale Beach (10 miles from Ft. Lauderdale/ Hollywood International Airport)
Phone ▼	(800) 327-1212, (954) 457-2000
Website ▼	www.Diplomatresort.com
Course ▼	Country Club at the Diplomat (18) – Joe Lee
Major Amenities ▼	Three restaurants
▼	Two lounges
▼	Private beach
▼	Marina
▼	Lagoon pool
▼	Tennis complex
Business Facilities ▼	225,000 square feet of meeting space
Nearby Attractions ▼	International Swimming Hall of Fame
▼	Museum of Discovery and Science Center and Blockbuster 3-D IMAX Theater
▼	Sawgrass Mills Outlet Mall
▼	Dania Antique Row
▼	Las Olas Boulevard shopping

▲   ▲   ▲

Don Shula's Hotel & Golf Club

WHAT'S IT LIKE to spend a golf vacation at Don Shula's Hotel & Golf Club? Don't fret—you won't be smashing into blocking dummies and running wind sprints while the former Miami Dolphins' coach barks orders from a towel. Far from it. Don Shula's Hotel & Golf Club, with its well-appointed accommodations and attentive service, is the opposite of what you would've found at a spartan, no-nonsense, Shula-style Dolphins' training camp. At times, there are lots of athletes at the resort, but they come mostly to regale in the comfy surroundings. The Dolphins and the University of Miami Hurricanes often stay at the hotel the night before a home game. Several NBA teams also stop over for shoot-a-rounds at the resort's fitness center when they're in Miami to play the Heat.

The resort complex is set in the five-square-mile village of Miami Lakes, one of the nation's first master-planned residential/resort communities. Lushly landscaped and bursting with tropical foliage at every turn, the community is self-contained, with many shops, restaurants, and outdoor cafés on Main Street, which serves as the town center for more than 25,000 residents.

Built in 1962, the course is a fully mature layout with large, shady live oak, palm, and fruit trees dotting a lake-laden landscape. Designed by Miami-based architect Bill Watts, the course has some of the highest elevated tees in south Florida and large undulating greens. Fifteen holes incorporate water in some fashion. In addition, the golf complex includes a lighted, eighteen-hole, par-3 executive course and a lighted range and practice area that is open until 11:00 P.M.

After a pleasant day on the links, ardent football fans and carnivores must visit Shula's Steak House, which overlooks the golf course. Part-restaurant, part-museum, Shula's is home to the original restaurant of what has become a very successful national chain. Shula's has been rated by several publications as one of the top ten steak houses in the nation. You won't find tofu or quiche in this place. Specialties at Shula's include certified Angus steaks grilled to perfection, fresh Florida seafood, and Maine lobster. Diners are surrounded by large, framed pictures of past Dolphin stars Bob Griese, Paul Warfield, and others from the 1972 17-0 perfect season, as well as all sorts of memorabilia from that year, including game balls, trophies, helmets, and Super Bowl rings.

Shula, the winningest coach in NFL history with 347 wins, provides the perfect antidote for those who have overstepped their caloric and cholesterol limits at his restaurant. His on-site Shula's Athletic Club, a popular workout haven for Miami's professional athletes, is a massive facility open to hotel guests, featuring a gymnasium with a regulation basketball court, an aerobics center, and racquetball courts.

Accommodations at the 205-room hotel include a mix of bi-level Lanai Suites, Junior Suites, and balconies overlooking gardens and the courtyard pool. The Golf Club's eighty-four rooms are targeted to the extended-stay traveler or anyone seeking more than a standard hotel room.

Things to Know	▼	***Don Shula's Hotel & Golf Club***
Location	▼	6842 Main Street, Miami Lakes
		(18 miles northwest of downtown Miami)
Phone	▼	(305) 821-1150, (800) 24-SHULA
Website	▼	www.donshulahotel.com
Courses	▼	Don Shula's Golf Club (18) –
		Bill Watts
	▼	Executive Course (9) – Bill Watts
Major Amenities	▼	Tennis
	▼	Swimming
	▼	Athletic club
	▼	Lighted par-3 course and driving range
	▼	Don Shula's Steak House
Business Facilities	▼	22,000 square feet of meeting space
Nearby Attractions	▼	Aventura Mall
	▼	Vizcaya Museum and Gardens
	▼	Calder Race Course
	▼	Pro Player Stadium

▲   ▲   ▲

Doral Golf Resort & Spa

THE BLUE MONSTER. No, it's not some wildly contorted roller coaster at a Florida theme park. Rather, it's one of the state's most famous golf courses, a rugged test that often leaves high-handicappers with that bleary-eyed look you see on roller coaster riders who have just been scared out of their Bermuda shorts. Site of the PGA Tour's Genuity Doral Championship, held in March, the Blue Monster was designed by Dick Wilson, then redesigned by Raymond Floyd in the mid-1990s. Floyd essentially put more teeth into the course by lengthening fairways, changing bunkers, and reshaping greens.

The Blue Monster's eighteenth hole, a 435-yard par-4, sweeps around a picturesque lake and is generally regarded as one of the most difficult finishing holes on the PGA Tour. Floyd has even called it the toughest par-4 in the world. With water on the left side from tee to green and a prevailing wind blowing across the fairway, you'd better hit your best drive of the day and an equally superb long-iron shot or it's bogey—make that double bogey—time.

A monster of a different sort is Doral's newest layout, the Greg Norman–designed Great White championship course. Norman has described it as a "desert-style" layout and it looks decidedly different from any other course in Florida. In place of rough, Norman used tightly packed coquina sand to frame fairways. Another trademark of the course is a series of pot bunkers that are characteristic of the courses Norman played growing up in his native Australia.

After you get through with either monster, blue or white (or it gets through with you), the other courses include the Red, a Dick

Wilson design with two island greens; the Gold, a Raymond Floyd restoration with water in play on every hole; and the Silver, which was recently renovated by Jerry Pate and is noted for its narrow fairways, moguls, and elevated target greens.

If your swing needs work, you're in the right place. The Jim McLean Golf School is a high-tech haven headed by PGA Teacher of the Year Jim McLean, whose client list includes Tom Kite, Steve Elkington, and Bruce Lietzke. One of McLean's recent innovations is a "Synergy Golf Conditioning" class that helps improve physical fitness on and off the course.

Aches and pains acquired from too many rounds of golf can be soothed at the 148,000-square-foot Spa at Doral, a plush European-inspired facility where health-related activities such as herbal wraps, mineral salt soaks, saunas, and Swiss showers are the order of the day. The spa also features forty-eight luxury suites, all with views of golf courses and lush gardens.

The 650-acre Doral Golf Resort & Spa has ten three- and four-story guest lodges housing 693 rooms and suites. Soft Caribbean colors abound, accented by marble bathrooms, marble-top bedside tables, plantation shutters, and bleached wood furniture.

Things to Know ▼ *Doral Golf Resort & Spa*

Location ▼ 4400 Northwest 87th Avenue, Miami
(7 miles west of Miami International
Airport)

Phone ▼ (305) 592-2000, (800) 9-DORAL-9

Website ▼ www.doralresort.com

Courses ▼ Blue Monster (18) – Dick Wilson

▼ Great White Course (18) – Greg Norman

▼ Red Course (18) – Dick Wilson

▼ Gold Course (18) – Raymond Floyd

▼ Silver Course (18) – Jerry Pate

Major Amenities ▼ Six restaurants and lounges

▼ European-style spa

▼ Eleven-court tennis center

▼ Four swimming pools including Blue
Lagoon with 125-foot water slide

▼ On-site boutique shopping

▼ Jim McLean Golf School

▼ Children's program

▼ Bicycle paths

▼ Bass fishing

Business Facilities ▼ 100,000 square feet of meeting space

Nearby Attractions ▼ Miami Art Deco Historic District

▼ Bayside Marketplace

▼ Vizcaya Museum and Gardens

▲   ▲   ▲

Palm Beach Polo & Country Club

WITH THIRTEEN POLO FIELDS and one of the nation's most comprehensive equestrian complexes, your polo horse will certainly feel at home at the Palm Beach Polo & Country Club, a 2,200-acre, luxury residential/resort community near West Palm Beach. Golfers will feel right at home as well. Palm Beach Polo has forty-five holes of championship golf that were designed by a marquee lineup of architects, including Pete and P. B. Dye, Ron Garl, Jerry Pate, and George Fazio.

The eighteen-hole Cypress Course wraps around the ninety-two-acre Big Blue Cypress Preserve. Designed by Pete Dye and his son P. B, the course has hallmark Dye features such as abrupt drop-offs around bunkers and mounds, huge bunkers paralleling lakes, and blind shots. One of the more exciting holes is the par-4 fourteenth, a 376-yard beauty that carries over a lake to a landing area, with a cypress tree in the center of the fairway.

The eighteen-hole Dunes Course, designed by Ron Garl and Jerry Pate, is a Scottish-style layout with extensive mounding, pot bunkers, grass traps, and fairways full of swales and ripples. For the casual golfer and those who want to sharpen their iron play, there is the fun-to-play, nine-hole Olde Course, designed by George Fazio.

Like polo and golf, tennis is taken seriously at Palm Beach Polo. Players can choose from three surfaces (hard, har-tru, and grass) and twenty-four courts (ten lighted). The complex features an amphitheater, championship courts, and two stadium grass courts. Other sports activities include croquet, squash, and racquetball. Guest lodging is clustered around or is adjacent to one of the resort's golf, polo, or tennis facilities. One- and two-story villas offer 120 units, including one-, two- and three-bedroom suites and studios.

Things to Know ▼	*Palm Beach Polo & Country Club*
Location ▼	11199 Polo Club Road, Wellington
Phone ▼	(561) 798-7000
Website ▼	www.pbpolo.com
Courses ▼	Cypress Course (18) – Pete Dye, P.B. Dye
▼	Dunes Course (18) – Jerry Pate, Ron Garl
▼	Olde Course (9) – George Fazio
Major Amenities ▼	Equestrian club and stable
▼	Thirteen polo fields
▼	Tennis and swim club
▼	Three clubhouses
▼	Championship croquet lawns
▼	Squash
▼	Racquetball
Business Facilities ▼	6,000 square feet of meeting space
Nearby Attractions ▼	Worth Avenue shopping district in Palm Beach
▼	Morikami Museum and Japanese Gardens
▼	Flagler Museum

▲   ▲   ▲

PGA National Resort & Spa

FOR GOLFAHOLICS WHO ARE BORDERLINE for a twelve-step program, one resort that can satisfy even the most voracious golf appetite is the PGA National Resort & Spa in Palm Beach Gardens. This 2,340-acre resort/residential community has not one, not two, not three, not four, but five championship golf courses.

Guests at the 339-room hotel are surrounded by palm-dotted golf holes and are a short walk from the front entrance to the headquarters building for the Professional Golfers Association of America. The five golf courses are designed by a star-studded lineup of architects: Jack Nicklaus, Tom Fazio, George Fazio, Arnold Palmer, and Karl Litten.

The headliner layout is the Champion Course, a long, tough course that opened in 1981 and was redesigned by Nicklaus in 1990. A previous host to the Ryder Cup and PGA Senior Championship, the course looks enticingly easy from some tees, where golfers hit to generously wide fairways. If you don't have a short game, however, get ready for a long, grueling five hours. Many of the greens are wildly undulating and are surrounded by all sorts of trouble, from deep bunkers to mounds and dark lagoons. When the wind starts to howl in the winter months, bring along two items—a windbreaker to protect against the chill and a calculator to add up additional strokes.

The Champion's fifteenth through seventeenth holes, which are called the "Bear Trap," comprise one of Florida's toughest stretches of finishing holes. The eighteenth is a double dogleg par-5 with water and bunkers on both sides of the snakelike fairway—a final, unforgettable farewell from Nicklaus.

Let's peruse the rest of the golf menu. The Palmer design, named the General, has a links feel. The Litten-designed Estate Course is used by the PGA of America as the primary site for their annual Club Professional Winter Tournament Program each year. The Squire Course is the resort's shortest layout, and the Haig Course is a high-handicapper's dream, with no cross-water hazards.

Wow, and you expect me to make anything less than a double bogey?

For both the uninitiated who want to join the dimple-ball set and long-time players desiring a tune-up for their swing, the Academy of Golf at PGA National can help golfers at both ends of the spectrum. Heading the academy is Mike Adams, one of Golf Magazine's Top 100 Teachers, whose philosophy is to treat every golfer seriously regardless of his or her skill level. His students have included tour professionals such as Michelle McGann, Jim Albus, Rick Fehr, and Bob Estes, as well as celebrities like Jack Nicholson and Michael Douglas.

Golf widows rejoice at PGA National's posh, 52,500-square-foot, European-style spa, which features more than one hundred services and the "Relaxing Waters of the World," an outdoor mineral pool filled with salts from the Dead Sea and the Salies de Bearn in the Pyrenees.

Topping the list of PGA National's eight restaurants and lounges are Shula's Steak House, where guests are surrounded by memorabilia from the Miami Dolphins' 1972 perfect season and are served telephone book–thick steaks, and Arezzo, a classy, northern Italian–style ristorante known for its re-creation of Michelangelo's Sistine Chapel painting on its ceiling.

PGA National has recently spent millions of dollars upgrading and revitalizing its guest rooms. Each room has a panoramic view of the lake, pool, or golf course. For apartment-style accommodations, each of the sixty-five cottage suites overlooking the golf course has two bedrooms, two full bathrooms, a large living room, a fully equipped kitchen, and a washer and dryer.

If you still want more golf after a few days at PGA National, you are (choose one):

A. A certifiable golfaholic

B. A professional golfer

C. Someone who really needs to broaden his/her interests

Things to Know ▼ *PGA National Resort & Spa*

Location ▼	400 Avenue of the Champions, Palm Beach Gardens (15 miles north of Palm Beach International Airport)
Phone ▼	(561) 627-2000, (800) 633-9150
Website ▼	www.pga-resorts.com
Courses ▼	Champion Course (18) – Jack Nicklaus
▼	General Course (18) – Arnold Palmer
▼	Estate Course (18) – Karl Litten
▼	Squire Course (18) – George Fazio, Tom Fazio
▼	Haig Course (18) – George Fazio, Tom Fazio
Major Amenities ▼	Eight restaurants and lounges
▼	Golf academy
▼	Tennis courts and swimming pools
▼	Spa
▼	Twenty-six-acre lake
▼	Croquet
▼	Health club
Business Facilities ▼	33,900 square feet of meeting space
Nearby Attractions ▼	Worth Avenue shopping district in Palm Beach
▼	Dreher Park Zoo
▼	Norton Gallery of Art
▼	Whitehall (Henry Flagler's estate)
▼	Raymond F. Kravis Center for the Performing Arts

▲   ▲   ▲

TPC at Heron Bay

IT'S HIGHLY UNLIKELY that any of us will score a touchdown at Lambeau Field, slug a home run into the upper deck of Yankee Stadium, or sink a game-winning free throw at Madison Square Garden. Yet tracing the strokes of our favorite golfers is attainable, as many of the courses on the PGA Tour are accessible to the public.

Some of the best to play are available through the PGA Tour's network of Tournament Players Clubs (TPCs), which is comprised of twenty-two clubs—eight daily-fee/resort clubs and fourteen private clubs—throughout the United States. Each TPC course was designed to serve as a host of a PGA or Senior PGA Tour annual event. The daily fee/resort TPCs are open to public play, and the private TPCs have memberships available by invitation or through sponsorship by another member or a PGA Tour player.

The TPC at Heron Bay in Coral Springs, site of the PGA Tour's Honda Classic, played in early March, has served as a spectacular venue for the event. Designed by PGA Tour member Mark McCumber, the course is designed over gently undulating terrain with numerous waterways and lakes that come into play frequently. Good putting is a prerequisite to scoring well at Heron Bay, which has mammoth, fast greens that average 7,000 square feet. (The average Tour green size is 6,000 square feet.) Playing close attention to club selection is equally important, especially during the winter and early spring, when the wind can sometimes blow ferociously. Unless you possess Tiger Woods' or John Daly's length, it is best to forget about where the pros hit from the tee. The championship tees are a whopping 7,360 yards, and the regular tees measure 6,300 yards. If you hit from the correct tees for your skill level, you're more likely to face the same approach shots the pros do.

TPC courses are legendary for their exciting and difficult finishing holes, which often elicit dramatic conclusions in tournaments. Heron Bay's eighteenth hole does not disappoint. The 450-yard, par-4 has water lining the entire right side of the fairway, and the approach shot must negotiate water and sand.

Don't be surprised to see all sorts of wildlife on the course. The TPC at Heron Bay is fully certified by the Audubon Cooperative Sanctuary Program, which was created to help golf course designers address pertinent environmental issues and make meaningful contributions to improve environmental quality. Among the wildlife spotted at Heron Bay are alligators, rabbits, foxes, opossums, raccoons, armadillos, and over fifty species of birds.

Amenities at Heron Bay include a spacious, tropical-style clubhouse that lies at the end of an avenue of one hundred tall royal palms; a state-of-the-art practice facility; and instruction by PGA professionals. Several major national chain hotels are located within fifteen miles of Heron Bay. For those who want to stay courseside, the Radisson Resort Coral Springs (954-753-5598) offers easy access and golf packages.

Things to Know ▼	***TPC at Heron Bay***
Location ▼	11775 Heron Bay Boulevard, Coral Springs (15 miles from downtown Ft. Lauderdale)
Phone ▼	(954) 796-2000, (800) 511-6616
Website ▼	www.playatpc.com
Course ▼	TPC at Heron Bay (18) – Mark McCumber
Major Amenities ▼	Addison Mizner style clubhouse
▼	Golf instruction
▼	PGA Tour–quality practice facility
Business Facilities ▼	Meeting and banquet space for up to 200 people
Nearby Attractions ▼	Sawgrass Mills Factory Outlet Mall
▼	Las Olas Boulevard
▼	International Swimming Hall of Fame
▼	Butterfly World

▲   ▲   ▲

Turnberry Isle Resort and Club

THE SIGHTS AND SOUNDS AT TURNBERRY are as much South of France as south Florida. Attracting an international clientele, including celebrity golfers Sylvester Stallone and Bill Clinton, the resort's Mediterranean-inspired architecture—combined with a secluded location on a private island on the Intracoastal Waterway—makes you feel as though you're staying at some trendy, isolated Côte d'Azur hideaway. Most guests forget they're just twenty-five miles north of downtown Miami in these 300 impeccably landscaped acres enveloped by tropical foliage.

While the setting is decidedly French Riviera—the buildings have stucco facades, terra cotta roofs, pillars, and arched promenades—the two eighteen-hole golf courses, named the North and South and designed by Robert Trent Jones Sr., are quintessentially American. Waterways wind gracefully through the layouts, and a prevailing wind tends to play havoc with club selection.

The more celebrated of the two courses is the South, which has hosted the Florida PGA Championship, Senior PGA and LPGA Tour events, and the annual Raymond Floyd Turnberry Isle Junior Classic. Dominated by superb par-5s and -3s, the course has a high-risk, high-reward personality. The straightforward 539-yard, par-5 sixth hole is an easy birdie for Tiger Woods or Davis Love III. The average resort player will need three solid shots, however, the final one over water to a medium-size green.

Even more challenging is the 545-yard, par-5 eighteenth, Turnberry's signature island hole. For those who dare to go for the green with a fairway wood on a second shot, the results are either heroic or disastrous. Getting a ball to stop on the green is a little like landing a hot-air balloon on the deck of an aircraft carrier. It's possible, but executing the feat is another matter.

The shorter North Course has narrow fairways and a picturesque front nine. Water comes into play on twelve holes, and there are strategically placed bunkers on every hole. The toughest hole is the 562-yard, par-5 fifth, which is framed on the entire right side by Lake Julius, named after one-time head pro and PGA Tour player Julius Boros.

Away from the courses, Turnberry's amenity menu was seemingly designed by golf widows. In addition to a new 25,000-square-foot, European-style spa with twenty-six treatment rooms, the complex includes two tennis centers with nineteen courts, a 117-slip marina with yacht charters and deep-sea fishing, a fitness center, and a private Ocean Club with beach, pool, cabanas, and

The views at Turnberry are awesome and so is the golf.

water sports. For shoppers, the sprawling Aventura Mall, anchored by Bloomingdale's, Macy's, and Lord and Taylor, is a three-minute walk across the street from the resort.

Despite the inevitable draw of the golf courses and other activities, leaving your room is harder than you think at Turnberry. The spacious rooms and suites are appointed with terra cotta floors, plush Oriental area rugs, blond wood furniture, and Italian marble. In-room amenities include walk-in closets and fresh-cut orchids. French doors open to flower-lined terraces with spectacular views of fairways and greens or pool gardens.

One good reason to leave the comfort of your room is the Veranda, Turnberry's award-winning dining room, selected as "the best gourmet dining experience in Miami" by the Zagat U.S. Hotel, Resort, and Spa Survey. Veranda's draw is an innovative cuisine called "Floribbean"—a fusion of south Florida's tropical flavors blended with Cuban, Caribbean, and Latin American influences.

Things to Know ▼	***Turnberry Isle Resort and Club***
Location ▼	19999 West Country Club Drive, Aventura (12 miles south of Ft. Lauderdale/Hollywood International Airport, 18 miles north of Miami International Airport)
Phone ▼	(305) 932-6200, (800) 327-7028
Website ▼	www.turnberryisle.com
Courses ▼	North Course (18) – Robert Trent Jones Sr.
▼	South Course (18) – Robert Trent Jones Sr.
Major Amenities ▼	Valet parking
▼	European-style spa
▼	Two tennis centers
▼	Private beach club along the Atlantic
▼	Two swimming pools
▼	Three-mile jogging path
▼	117-slip marina
Business Facilities ▼	Meeting and banquet space for up to 200 people
Nearby Attractions ▼	Aventura Mall
▼	Bal Harbour Shops
▼	Pari-mutuel horse racing at Calder Race Course
▼	South Beach

▲   ▲   ▲

Southwest

1. The Resort at Longboat Key Club
2. Sunstream Hotels & Resorts
3. South Seas Resort
4. Hyatt Regency Coconut Point Resort & Spa
5. Naples Beach Hotel & Golf Club
6. The Registry Resort
7. Ritz-Carlton Golf Resort, Naples
8. Marco Island Marriott Resort & Golf Club

7 Southwest

Hyatt Regency Coconut Point Resort & Spa

DURING HIS PRIME ON THE PGA TOUR, Raymond Floyd had a reputation as an assassin when he got the lead in a tournament. Winner of the 1976 Masters, 1986 U.S. Open, and 1969 and 1981 PGA Championship, Floyd had a thorough and calculating style that would discourage the rest of the field from thinking they had a chance to overcome him. Luckily, Floyd the golf designer is a kinder, gentler sort who doesn't try to defeat the golfers who play his courses. His twenty-seven-hole layout at the Hyatt Regency

Coconut Point Resort & Spa in Bonita Springs is a fair, fun, and playable course.

Situated contiguous to Estero Bay, the course is the centerpiece amenity for the luxury resort that opened in September 2001. Known as one of the best trouble-shot players in the game, Floyd is certainly cognizant that most resort course players don't share the same skill. With that in mind, the course has no high rough or formal bunkers. The innovative design challenges with large, sandy waste areas and perched greens. For errant approach shots, there are numerous collection areas around the greens that require solid short-game execution. Water comes into play on more than half of the holes.

The 450-room, eighteen-story Hyatt Regency Coconut Point Resort & Spa is part of Pelican Landing, a master-planned community developed by WCI Communities, one of Florida's largest community developers and homebuilders. Like other resorts in Hyatt Hotel's golf portfolio, which includes seven other golf resorts in Florida and the Caribbean (Orlando, Key West, Aruba, Grand Cayman, Dorado Beach and Cerromar Beach, Puerto Rico, and St. Lucia), Coconut Point is laden with outstanding amenities.

Away from the course, there is a wealth of recreational options at Coconut Point, starting with a spectacular 4,000-square-foot pool and children's lagoon with a slide, lap pools, and waterfall pool with grand fountain. In total, the property has access to four outdoor swimming pools as well as a private island beach. To soothe aching muscles after a round of golf, Coconut Point has an 18,000-square-foot fitness center and full-service European spa that offers treatment and massage rooms as well as aerobic, cardiovascular, and strength-training equipment. Other amenities include three restaurants, four har-tru tennis courts, a marina, a retail shop, a beauty and sundries shop, and Camp Hyatt, Hyatt's renowned children's program.

Things to Know ▼	*Hyatt Regency Coconut Point*
Location ▼	5001 Coconut Road, Bonita Springs (midway between Ft. Myers and Naples one mile west of U.S. 41)
Phone ▼	(941) 992-9850
Website ▼	www.coconutpoint.hyatt.com
Courses ▼	Hyatt Regency Coconut Point Resort & Spa Resort Course (27) – Raymond Floyd
Major Amenities ▼	Hyatt-signature landscaped swimming pool
▼	Fitness center and spa
▼	Private island beach
▼	Three restaurants
▼	Four tennis courts
Business Facilities ▼	30,000 square feet of indoor meeting space; 20,000 square feet of outdoor meeting space
Nearby Attractions ▼	Eco-tours on Estero Bay
▼	Naples Philharmonic Center for the Arts
▼	Thomas Edison Winter Home and Museum
▼	Broadway Palm Dinner Theater

▲   ▲   ▲

Marco Island Marriott Resort & Golf Club

AS ONE OF APPROXIMATELY EIGHTY nationwide, fully certified members of the Audubon Cooperative Sanctuary Program, the Marco Island Marriott Golf Club is as much an eco-adventure as it is a golf experience. Weaving through forests of pine and palm trees, lagoons, marshes, and swamps, the golf course serves as a habitat for wildlife like the gopher tortoise, brown bat, alligator, and black bear.

The fairways are rimmed by towering pines and banked by malaluka grasses (similar to bamboo) and Brazilian pepper trees. Water comes into play on fifteen holes in the form of snaking waterways and dew-soaked bogs, with a series of wooden bridges to guide players over eight large lakes. In addition to the natural hazards, designer Joe Lee fashioned four bulkheaded greens and seventy-four bunkers to provide more challenge. The most ominous hazard, however, is the deceptive winds that blow from the northeast and play havoc with club selection.

Luckily, if you don't have your "A" game (or have never had an "A" game), help is not far away. The club's extensive practice area has six putting greens and a fourteen-acre learning facility. Marco Island Marriott Golf Club is one of the designated sites of the John Jacobs' School of Golf, the largest of all golf schools worldwide. Founded in 1971 by former British Ryder Cup captain John Jacobs and PGA professional Shelby Futch, the program offers practical, straightforward, results-oriented instruction that focuses primarily on analyzing the swing plane and developing consistency. Golf schools range from weekend sessions to seven-day programs.

A few miles away, the 735-room hotel sits on a three-and-a-half-mile stretch of uninterrupted Gulf of Mexico Beach surrounded by gardens brimming with pink hibiscus and bright red and purple begonias. The lobby is a vaulted atrium with three-story picture windows, marble floors, coquina rock pillars, and a garden courtyard. All guest rooms and suites feature private balconies and interiors appointed in tropical motifs with heavy emphasis on turquoise and soft reds. In addition, there are thirty beach and poolside lanai suites with exclusive outdoor access.

To become a full-fledged albeit temporary participant in the laid-back, sunset-watching, piña-colada-drinking Marco Island lifestyle, the resort's Quinn's on the Beach restaurant is one of the most happening restaurants on the island. Overflowing with maritime memorabilia such as hollowed-tree canoes, spinning ships' wheels, cargo nets, and carved-wood sea creatures, Quinn's has all the obligatory local favorites, like Florida grouper and Key lime pie. Quinn's throws weekly beachside bashes with entertainment ranging from New Orleans jazz and country western to jazz-fusion and '50s rock 'n' roll.

Can I borrow one . . . two . . . no, make that three balls?

Things to Know ▼	*Marco Island Marriott Resort*
Location ▼	400 South Collier Boulevard, Marco Island (25 miles south of Naples)
Phone ▼	(941) 394-2511, (800) 438-4373
Website ▼	www.marriotthotels.com/mrkfl
Course ▼	Marco Island Marriott Golf Club (18) – Joe Lee
Major Amenities ▼	John Jacobs' Golf School
▼	Sixteen-court tennis complex
▼	Three swimming pools
▼	Spa
▼	Miniature golf
▼	Five restaurants
▼	Four lounges
Business Facilities ▼	50,000 square feet of meeting space
Nearby Attractions ▼	Island trolley tour
▼	Shelling and sightseeing cruises
▼	Shopping in Naples
▼	Everglades National Park

▲   ▲   ▲

Naples Beach Hotel & Golf Club

FOR THOSE IN SEARCH of the quintessential southwest Florida golf experience, the Naples Beach Hotel & Golf Club is ideally situated to pursue activities like shell-hunting, sunset-watching, and golf (a thirty-second commute between the beach and the course). A solid wedge shot across the street from the front lobby is the eighteen-hole championship golf course, and the back of the hotel is fringed by 1,000 feet of sandy Gulf of Mexico shoreline.

Built in 1929 and later redesigned by golf architect Ron Garl, the golf course has received several enhancements in the past few years. Rated by Golf for Women magazine as among the "100 Most Women-Friendly Clubs," the Naples Beach Golf Club plays host to the Florida State Senior Men's Open Championship. The course is well bunkered: Garl has placed bunkers strategically so that a mistake in club selection or an erratic approach shot will cost golfers dearly.

Owned and operated by the Watkins family for more than fifty years, the Naples Beach Hotel & Golf Club is the kind of sophisticated yet folksy hotel that once dominated Florida's coasts before skyscraper condos and major hotel chains arrived. In 1950, Henry B. Watkins Sr., a successful toy manufacturer in Columbus, Ohio, became inspired by the vacation potential of southwest Florida. He leased a few hundred acres of beachfront property in Naples, including an abandoned eighteen-hole golf course. Today, Watkins' grandson Michael serves as president and part-owner (with his mother and his brother, Henry B. Watkins III). It is a resort that pays homage to its Old Florida roots yet is constantly being updated to assure patrons of its quality and luxury.

Life's a beach in Naples.

In 1999, the resort debuted a lavish 22,000-square-foot clubhouse and spa overlooking the golf course. The spa, which serves as the golf and recreation hub, offers massage therapies; skin, hair, and beauty treatments; a complete fitness facility; an aerobics studio; and personal trainers. In the clubhouse, the men's and women's locker rooms feature a steam room, saunas, and a whirlpool.

The 318-room hotel has 274 guest rooms, all with furnished balconies, and 44 one-bedroom suites that have a separate living room, dining area, kitchen, and other amenities. All rooms have a view of either the Gulf of Mexico or the golf course. Aside from tennis and host of water sports, a popular pastime for patrons is shopping at the chic boutiques and art galleries in downtown Naples, a five-minute drive from the resort.

Things to Know ▼	*Naples Beach Hotel & Golf Club*
Location ▼	851 Gulf Shore Boulevard North, Naples (40 miles from Southwest Florida International Airport)
Phone ▼	(941) 261-2222, (800) 866-1946
Website ▼	www.NaplesBeachHotel.com
Course ▼	Naples Beach Hotel & Golf Club Resort Course (18) – Ron Garl
Major Amenities ▼	White-sand beach
▼	Four restaurants and lounges
▼	Swimming pool
▼	On-site shops
▼	Full-service spa
▼	Complimentary children's program
▼	Six tennis courts
▼	Bicycle rentals
Business Facilities ▼	34,000 square feet of meeting space
Nearby Attractions ▼	Tin City shopping/restaurant complex
▼	Naples Philharmonic Center for the Arts
▼	Everglades National Park

▲   ▲   ▲

The Registry Resort

WHEN YOU BOOK YOUR ACCOMMODATIONS at the Registry Resort in Naples, you'll receive a luxurious room or suite in an eighteen-story tower with a private balcony overlooking the Gulf of Mexico. Equally rewarding for golfers is the opportunity to play Naples Grande Golf Club, one of southwest Florida's best private golf courses.

Designed by Rees Jones, Naples Grande was built by Florida billionaire H. Wayne Huizenga's Boca Resorts hotel company, which owns the 474-room Registry Resort and nearby 124-suite Edgewater Beach Hotel. As a result, blocks of tee times are reserved for guests of both hotels. Better still, resort guest golfers are treated just as cordially and attentively as regular members. While some private clubs treat resort guests as high-paying trespassers, Naples Grande, because of its unique ownership situation, allows visitors to totally immerse themselves in the private-club experience.

A ten-minute drive from the Registry, Naples Grande, which opened in 1999, is the antithesis of the real estate–driven golf course so prominent in Naples, one of Florida's fastest growing communities. Naples Grande has no pools, tennis courts, or homes framing the fairways. Costing more than $10 million to build, the course is exquisitely maintained to Augusta National–level standards.

Rees Jones, known for his redesign work on several major championship courses such as Baltusrol, Congressional, Pinehurst (No. 2), and Brookline, worked diligently to create a course decidedly different from any other in Naples. He succeeded. Although routed out of the same hammock swamps that define this corner of Florida, Naples Grande boasts a babbling brook that comes into play on three holes, a thirty-acre lake, and greens raised on waterside cliffs.

When you arrive at Naples Grande, your clubs are unloaded for you in the parking lot. Then the course ranger delivers a friendly, pre-round monologue about fixing divots and keeping the pace of play moving along. Then you hit a few balls at the range, where pyramids of Titleist balls wait at each station. Following your round of golf, several attendants will descend upon your cart, clean your clubs, then exaggerate how well you must have done on the course and prepare you for your return to the hotel.

Enhancing the golf experience at the Registry is the resort's on-site golf concierge. A knowledgeable golf professional, he keeps a lending library of reference books and instructional videos available and furnishes inside knowledge about Naples Grande and other courses in the Naples area. For the guest who had not planned to play golf but suddenly decides he can't leave without teeing up at least once, the golf concierge can take care of everything, from a glove and tees to balls and rental clubs.

Hazards, hazards everywhere at Naples Grande.

The resort's golf shop is located adjacent to the lobby, a great place to sip a cool drink and spin golf stories. The classy Lobby Lounge, smartly paneled in driftwood-colored oak and sporting floors made of Italian marble adorned with Oriental carpets, provides a comfortable and refined setting. Among the other resort highlights are the Lafite, a gourmet dining room with a superb wine list; a boardwalk that snakes its way through a mangrove to the beach; an award-winning children's program; an expansive pool complex with natural rock formations, waterslide, and private cabanas; and a Visiting Artist Series Gallery, which brings world-renowned artists to the property.

Things to Know ▼	*The Registry Resort*
Location ▼	475 Seagate Drive, Naples
Phone ▼	(941) 597-3232, (800) 247-9810
Website ▼	www.registryresort.com
Course ▼	Naples Grande Golf Club (18) – Rees Jones
Major Amenities ▼	Five swimming pools
▼	200-acre mangrove forest
▼	Fifteen tennis courts
▼	Five restaurants
▼	Health club
▼	Boutique shopping
Business Facilities ▼	45,000 square feet of meeting space
Nearby Attractions ▼	Naples Philharmonic Center for the Arts
▼	Waterside Shops (one block away)
▼	Corkscrew Swamp Sanctuary

▲   ▲   ▲

The Resort at Longboat Key Club

MORE THAN 400 YEARS AGO, Spanish explorer Hernando de Soto landed with his men in their longboats on what is now called Longboat Key, a barrier island near Sarasota. If Señor de Soto were to magically return today, he would be pleasantly surprised to find a sophisticated, 1,000-acre resort prepared to pamper him and his crew and provide some much-needed R and R from his rugged explorer duties.

The Resort at Longboat Key Club, accessible via a causeway from Sarasota, is a private club and resort/residential community bordered on the west by the Gulf of Mexico and on the east by Sarasota Bay. Residents and guests relish the quiet, secluded ambience and the flawless white sands of the Gulf of Mexico, yet civilization is just minutes away at St. Armands Circle, a European-style, outdoor shopping plaza with international shops, restaurants, and galleries.

For the golfer, there are forty-five holes that take full advantage of the wide, sugar-white, quartz-sand beach and tropical foliage. The Islandside Course, designed by Bill Mitchell in 1960, borders the Gulf of Mexico and has water in play on every hole. Narrow, deceptively long fairways lined with over five thousand palm trees and stunning pink and white blooming oleander thread throughout lakes and lagoons, making the layout an acknowledged test in accuracy. Ever-present Gulf breezes, which seem to shift from hole to hole as the course changes direction, are a hazard themselves and have blown many tee shots into watery graves.

The Harbourside Course, which is actually three nine-hole courses, is a completely different experience from the Islandside. Situated a few miles from the resort alongside Sarasota Bay, the Harbourside weaves through stands of palmetto, Southern pine, live oak, and several varieties of palm and fig trees. It's a good idea to dial down your power game on this track. Water and bunkers rim most of the fairways as well as the greens, creating a target golf experience where big hitters had better hit to a safe spot or they'll be sorry.

For those who are admitted sorry golfers and for low-hand-icappers too, the resort's golf school is headed by David Matthews, a twenty-year class "A" member of the PGA. Highlighting the curriculum is analysis on the "Computer Coach" system, which gives players the opportunity to have their swings recorded on video, then digitized by computer.

When the clubs are put away for the day, golfers return to luxurious vacation accommodations. The multi-story complex of 232 rooms and suites ranges from guest rooms to two-bedroom suites. Views are magnificent from every unit, with balconies overlooking the Gulf of Mexico or the many lagoons of the Islandside Course. Most rooms have full kitchens, washers and dryers, and living/dining areas.

Things to Know ▼	***The Resort at Longboat Key Club***
Location ▼	301 Gulf of Mexico Drive, Longboat Key (3 miles from downtown Sarasota)
Phone ▼	(941) 383-8821, (800) 237-8821
Website ▼	www.longboatkeyclub.com
Courses ▼	Islandside Course (18) – Bill Mitchell
▼	Harbourside Course (27) – Willard Byrd
Major Amenities ▼	Private beach
▼	Four restaurants
▼	Fully equipped fitness center
▼	Thirty-eight tennis courts
▼	Children's program
▼	Biking
▼	Sailing
▼	Fishing
Business Facilities ▼	Can accommodate groups of 10 to 150
Nearby Attractions ▼	St. Armands Circle shopping area
▼	John and Mable Ringling Museum of Art
▼	Mote Marine Aquarium
▼	Marie Selby Botanical Gardens

▲   ▲   ▲

Ritz-Carlton Golf Resort, Naples

FLORIDA'S NEWEST GOLF RESORT, the 295-room Ritz-Carlton Golf Resort, opened in December 2001 inside the gates of a 700-acre golf community called Tiburon. Every room and suite at the resort has a private balcony with a golf course view. Marble and elegant wood treatments are used generously in the lobby, common areas, and guest rooms. In true Ritz-Carlton fashion, the in-room amenities are plentiful, highlighted by marble bathrooms, plush bathrobes, and European toiletries. For the business traveler, there is twenty-four-hour secretarial service and even a technology butler on call.

The thirty-six hole Tiburon Golf Club, designed by Greg Norman, sits just outside the doors of the hotel. It's a target-style layout with—get ready to cheer, high-handicappers—no rough. Or at least no rough in the conventional sense. Fairways at Tiburon (Spanish for "shark") are lined with pine straw instead of high grass, with the highest rough maintained at a fairway height of one-half inch. Other course features include tangerine-colored coquina sand in bunkers, stacked-sod wall bunkers, native habitat bordering fairways, and forced carries over water and wetlands. In addition, there are a 30,000-square-foot clubhouse and the Rick Smith Golf Academy.

Next to golf, shopping is high on the list of desired activities for guests staying at the hotel. Ten minutes from the resort complex are two, upscale, uniquely designed shopping centers: the Mediterranean-style Village on Venetian Bay and the Waterside Shops.

Things to Know ▼	*Ritz-Carlton Golf Resort, Naples*
Location ▼	2600 Tiburon Drive, Naples (29 miles from Southwest Florida International Airport)
Phone ▼	(941) 593-2000, (800) 241-3333
Website ▼	www.ritzcarlton.com
Course ▼	Tiburon Golf Club (36) – Greg Norman
Major Amenities ▼	Two restaurants
▼	Cigar bar
▼	Ritz Kids Program
▼	Valet parking
▼	Fitness center
▼	Four tennis courts
▼	Heated outdoor pool
▼	Twice-daily housekeeping
▼	Rick Smith Golf Academy
Business Facilities ▼	15,000 square feet of meeting space
Nearby Attractions ▼	Naples Philharmonic Center for the Arts
▼	Corkscrew Swamp Sanctuary
▼	Waterside Shops
▼	Fifth and Third Street South shopping district

▲   ▲   ▲

South Seas Resort

SOUTH SEAS RESORT occupies 330 acres at the northern tip of Captiva Island, a barrier island seven miles west of Ft. Myers. Enveloped by lush tropical foliage and rimmed by stunning white sand and turquoise water, the island could easily pass as some secluded Caribbean hideaway.

Not surprisingly, Captiva Island has the legacy of being a secret enclave to get away from it all. According to legend, the island's natural splendor first caught the attention of pirates seeking sanctuary between raids. During the latter half of the 1700s and into the early 1800s, the many coves and hidden bays of Captiva and adjacent Sanibel Island harbored ships and ragged crews. The name Captiva apparently came about because a pirate named José Gaspar kept his women captive here, or so legend has it. The island's birth as a vacation spot didn't begin until 1900, when Clarence Chadwick, inventor of the check writer machine, acquired the north end of Sanibel and all of Captiva Island.

There is barely enough room on the tiny island for a nine-hole golf course, and most visiting golfers are understandably skeptical about the layout. Visions of a pitch-and-putt course with tiny greens, flat bunkers, and one tee placement per hole probably flash through their minds. But Redfish Point, South Seas' nine-hole course, undeniably destroys that stereotype. The 3,100-yard, par-36 course has a couple of "air it out" par-5s, challenging par-3s, and awesome views of the Gulf of Mexico. Nowhere in Florida will you find a resort nine-hole course with such character and beauty. South Seas guests are also afforded play privileges at The Dunes Golf & Tennis Club, an eighteen-hole course on Sanibel Island designed by PGA Tour player Mark McCumber. "Water, water everywhere" is a good way to describe this layout, which has water hazards on sixteen holes.

Oh, brother, I'm going to owe these guys some money.

Following a round of golf, if you can't find anything to do
at South Seas, you're basically a hopeless couch potato. For those
who fit that bill: don't worry, you can still get cable TV at this
amenity-rich resort. For water sports enthusiasts, South Seas offers
seemingly every imaginable way to enjoy the Gulf of Mexico. It
features sailing, windsurfing, fishing, water skiing, scuba diving,
and shell-collecting. You can also rent a boat and take an excursion
to nearby islands. You'll never be far from a pool—the resort has
eighteen scattered throughout the property.

Dining at South Seas ranges from candlelight to casual. The
offerings include King's Crown Restaurant, which combines an elegant, waterfront setting and an award-winning culinary team;
Chadwick's, known for its lavish Sunday champagne brunch; The
Porter House, where aged steaks and an extensive wine selection
are the draw; and Cap'n Al's Seafood Grill, a popular spot for dining
alfresco and watching luxury yachts cruise by in the marina.

The resort's 600 accommodations, which encompass hotel rooms, villas, beach cottages, and private homes, feature beach, bay, marina, tennis center, and golf course views.

Things to Know ▼	*South Seas Resort*
Location ▼	5400 Plantation Road, Captiva Island (7 miles off coast of Ft. Myers)
Phone ▼	(941) 472-5111, (800) 237-6000
Website ▼	www.south-seas-resort.com
Course ▼	Redfish Point (9) – Jerry Heard
Major Amenities ▼	Seven restaurants and lounges
▼	Seventeen boutiques and shops
▼	Eighteen swimming pools
▼	Two and a half miles of beach
▼	Nineteen tennis courts
▼	Charter boats for fishing and sailing
▼	Sailing school
▼	Children's recreation program
▼	Nature center
▼	On-site marina
Business Facilities ▼	30,000 square feet of meeting space
Nearby Attractions ▼	Sanibel Island
▼	Cayo Costa Island State Preserve
▼	J. N. "Ding" Darling National Wildlife Refuge
▼	Chadwick's shopping center

▲   ▲   ▲

Sunstream Hotels & Resorts

FT. MYERS BEACH–BASED Sunstream Hotels & Resorts has a portfolio of six resorts in the area. On or near the beach, the properties are well managed and provide guests with first-class accommodations and amenities at affordable rates. Sunstream properties don't have on-site golf courses. However, the company has forged close working relationships with several Ft. Myers courses, and play arrangements are made easily.

For those who would like to incorporate eco-tourism with a golf getaway, all of Sunstream's properties are situated only a few miles from popular nature-based activities. Among the activities are kayak and canoe expeditions to historical Mound Key; guided tours to view sea turtles, manatees, and dolphins in their natural habitat; shelling excursions; swamp buggy tours through the Telegraph Cypress Swamp to view alligators, birds, and wild turkeys; and bird-watching trips.

Sunstream's flagship property is the 124-suite Diamondhead All-Suite Beach Resort, a twelve-story tower that sits directly on Ft. Myers Beach. Each of the suites has 700 square feet of living area, a fully equipped kitchen, and two telephones with data ports. Nearby, the Gullwing Beach Resort is Sunstream's newest property. On a quiet stretch of beach, the eleven-story resort has sixty-six one-, two- and three-bedroom suites with private, screened lanais, Jacuzzi tubs, and fully appointed kitchens.

Recreational options include a beachfront swimming pool, cabanas, a hot tub, a picnic gazebo, a barbecue area, tennis courts, a gift shop, and a fitness center. A few blocks away from both properties, the par-61 Bay Beach Golf Club affords playing privileges to Sunstream guests. Another course available for play is Kelly Greens Golf Course, five miles away.

Other resorts in Sunstream's portfolio include the sixty-suite Pointe Estero All-Suite Resort, the sixty-suite Santa Maria All-Suite Resort, the 104-room Grand View, and the 156-room Park Shore Resort. Sunstream has an exceptional, easy-to-navigate website that constantly features special room rate deals and packages.

The sandy environs on Fort Myers Beach.

Things to Know ▼	*Sunstream Hotels & Resorts*
Location ▼	6620 Estero Boulevard, Ft. Myers Beach
Phone ▼	(941) 765-4111, (888) 627-5151
Website ▼	www.sunstream.com
Courses ▼	Kelly Greens – Gordon Lewis
▼	Bay Beach Golf Club – Fred Conrad
Major Amenities ▼	Beachside properties with numerous water sports recreation options
▼	Seventeen boutiques and shops
▼	Eighteen swimming pools
▼	Two and a half miles of beach
▼	Nineteen tennis courts
▼	Charter boats for fishing and sailing
▼	Sailing school
▼	Children's recreation program
▼	Nature center
▼	On-site marina
Business Facilities ▼	6,000 square feet of meeting space (Diamondhead); groups up to 60 people (Gullwing)
Nearby Attractions ▼	Everglades Day Safari
▼	Koreshan State Park
▼	Greyhound dog racing
▼	John Burroughs Home

▲　　　▲　　　▲

Category Listings

Multiple Golf Courses

Amelia Island Plantation Resort 31
Arnold Palmer's Bay Hill Club &
    Lodge 51
Bluewater Bay 15
ChampionsGate 57
Club Med Sandpiper Village 105
Doral Golf Resort & Spa 140
Grand Cypress Resort 60
Grenelefe Golf & Tennis Resort 63
Hyatt Regency Coconut Point Resort &
    Spa 157
LPGA International 112
Marriott's Bay Point Resort Village 20
Mission Inn Golf & Tennis Resort 69
Orange County National Golf Center &
    Lodge 73
Palm Beach Polo & Country Club 143
Palm Coast Resort 114
PGA National Resort & Spa 145
PGA Village 117
Ponte Vedra Inn & Club 37
The Resort at Longboat Key Club 169
Resort at Sandestin 24
Ritz-Carlton Golf Resort, Naples 172
Saddlebrook Resort 91
Sawgrass Marriott Resort 42
Turnberry Isle Resort & Club 152
Walt Disney World 78
Westin Innisbrook Resort 96
World Golf Village 46

Beachside

Amelia Island Plantation Resort 31
The Breakers 131
Edgewater Beach Resort 18
Marco Island Marriott Resort & Golf
    Club 160
Naples Beach Hotel & Golf Club 163
Ponte Vedra Inn & Club 37
The Registry Resort 166
The Resort at Longboat Key Club 169

Resort at Sandestin 24
Ritz-Carlton, Amelia Island 40
South Walton County 27
Space Coast 120
Sunstream Hotels & Resorts 177
Tradewinds Island Resorts 94
The Westin Diplomat Resort & Spa 134

Romantic

The Biltmore Hotel 125
Boca Raton Resort & Club 128
The Breakers 131
The Registry Resort 166
Renaissance Vinoy Resort 88
Ritz-Carlton, Amelia Island 40
Ritz-Carlton, Naples 172
South Seas Resort 174
Turnberry Isle Resort & Club 152

Children's Programs

Amelia Plantation Resort 31
The Biltmore Hotel 125
Boca Raton Resort & Club 128
The Breakers 131
Club Med Sandpiper Village 105
Doral Golf Resort & Spa 140
Grand Cypress Resort 60
Hyatt Regency Coconut Point Resort &
    Spa 157
Marco Island Marriott Resort & Golf
    Club 160
Marriott's Bay Point Resort Village 20
Mission Inn Golf & Tennis Resort 69
Naples Beach Hotel & Golf Club 163
Orlando World Center Marriott 76
PGA National Resort & Spa 145
The Registry Resort 166
Renaissance Vinoy Resort 88
The Resort at Longboat Key Club 169
Resort at Sandestin 24
Ritz-Carlton, Amelia Island 40
Ritz-Carlton Golf Resort, Naples 172

Saddlebrook Resort 91
Sawgrass Marriott Resort 42
South Seas Resort 174
Sunstream Hotels & Resorts 177
Tradewinds Island Resorts 94
Turnberry Isle Resort & Club 169
Walt Disney World 78
The Westin Diplomat Resort & Spa 134
Westin Innisbrook Resort 96

Tennis

Amelia Island Plantation Resort 31
Boca Raton Resort & Club 128
The Breakers 131
Club Med Sandpiper Village 105
Doral Golf Resort & Spa 140
Grand Cypress Resort 60
Grenelefe Golf & Tennis Resort 63
Mission Inn Golf & Tennis Resort 69
PGA National Resort & Spa 145
Saddlebrook Resort 91
Sawgrass Marriott Resort 42
South Seas Resort 174
The Westin Diplomat Resort & Spa 134
Westin Innisbrook Resort 96

Full-Service Spa

Amelia Island Plantation Resort 31
The Biltmore Hotel 125
Boca Raton Resort & Club 128
The Breakers 131
Don Shula's Hotel & Golf Club 137
Doral Golf Resort & Spa 140
Hyatt Regency Coconut Point Resort & Spa 157
Naples Beach Hotel & Golf Club 163
Palm Beach Polo & Country Club 143
PGA National Resort & Spa 145
Ponte Vedra Inn & Club 37
The Registry Resort 166
Renaissance Vinoy Resort 88
Saddlebrook Resort 91
Turnberry Isle Resort & Club 152
Walt Disney World 78
The Westin Diplomat Resort & Spa 134

Near Theme Parks

Celebration 54
ChampionsGate 57
Grand Cypress Resort 60
Orange County National Golf Center & Lodge 73
Orlando World Center Marriott 76
Saddlebrook Resort 91
Walt Disney World 78

Near Outlet Shopping

Arnold Palmer's Bay Hill Club & Lodge 51
Celebration 54
ChampionsGate 57
Don Shula's Hotel & Golf Club 137
Grand Cypress Resort 60
Orlando World Center Marriott 76
Palm Coast Resort 114
Resort at Sandestin 24
Walt Disney World 78
World Golf Village 46

Equestrian Facilities

Grand Cypress Resort 60
Palm Beach Polo & Country Club 143

PGA Tour Tournament Venues

Arnold Palmer's Bay Hill Club & Lodge: Bay Hill Invitational (March) 51
Doral Golf Resort & Spa: Genuity Championship (February) 140
Sawgrass Marriott Resort: The Players Championship (March) 42
TPC at Heron Bay: Honda Classic (March) 149
Walt Disney World: National Car Rental Classic at Walt Disney World Resort (October) 78
Westin Innisbrook Resort: Tampa Bay Classic (September) 96
World Golf Village: Liberty Mutual Legends of Golf/Senior PGA Tour (April) 46

Exceptional Gourmet Dining

The Biltmore Hotel (La Palme d'Or) 125
Boca Raton Resort & Club (27 Ocean Blue) 128
The Breakers (L'Escalier) 131
Grand Cypress Resort (Black Swan) 60
Registry Resort (Lafite) 166
Renaissance Vinoy Resort (Marchand's Grill) 88
Ritz-Carlton, Amelia Island (The Grill) 40
Sawgrass Marriott Resort (Augustine Grille) 42
South Seas Resort (King's Crown) 174
Turnberry Isle Resort & Club (The Veranda) 152

Thick Steaks and Martinis

The Breakers (Flagler Steak House) 131
The Westin Diplomat Resort & Spa (Marty's) 134
Don Shula's Hotel & Golf Club (Don Shula's Steak House) 137
PGA National Resort & Spa (Don Shula's Steak House) 145
Renaissance Vinoy Resort (Fred's Bar) 88
Saddlebrook (Dempsey's) 91
Walt Disney World/WDW Swan and Dolphin Hotel (Don Shula's Steak House) 78
Westin Innisbrook Resort (DY's) 96

Boating/Sailing (On-site Marinas)

Bluewater Bay 15
Boca Raton Resort & Club 128
Club Med Sandpiper Village 105
The Westin Diplomat Resort & Spa 134
Marriott's Bay Point Resort Village 20
Palm Coast Resort 114
Plantation Inn & Golf Resort 86

Renaissance Vinoy Resort 88
Resort at Sandestin 24
Turnberry Isle Resort & Club 152

RVs Welcome

The Great Outdoors 110

Golf Course Architects

Bill Amick
Palm Coast Resort 114

Pete Dye
Amelia Island Plantation Resort 31
Palm Beach Polo & Country Club 143
PGA Village 117
Walt Disney World 78

Tom Fazio
Amelia Island Plantation Resort 31
Bluewater Bay 15
PGA National Resort & Spa 145
PGA Village 117
Walt Disney World 78
World Woods Golf Club 100

Raymond Floyd
Doral Golf Resort & Spa 140
Hyatt Regency Coconut Point Resort &
Spa 157

Ron Garl
The Great Outdoors 110
Grenelefe Golf & Tennis Resort 63
Naples Beach Hotel & Golf Club 163
Palm Beach Polo & Country Club 143
Renaissance Vinoy Resort 88

Arthur Hills
LPGA International 112

Rees Jones
LPGA International 112
Resort at Sandestin 24

Robert Trent Jones Jr.
Celebration 54

Robert Trent Jones Sr.
Boca Raton Resort & Club 128
Grenelefe Golf & Tennis Resort 63

Ponte Vedra Inn & Club 37
Turnberry Isle Resort & Club 152

Gary Koch
Mission Inn Golf & Tennis Resort 69

Joe Lee
Boca Raton Resort & Club 128
The Westin Diplomat Resort & Spa 134
Marco Island Marriott Resort & Golf
Club 160
Orlando World Center Marriott 76
Ponte Vedra Inn & Club 37
Walt Disney World 78

Mark Mahanna
Club Med Sandpiper Village 105
Plantation Inn & Golf Resort 86

Mark McCumber
TPC at Heron Bay 149

Jack Nicklaus
Grand Cypress Resort 60
Palm Coast Resort 114
PGA National Resort & Spa 145
World Golf Village 46

Greg Norman
ChampionsGate 57
Doral Golf Resort & Spa 140
Ritz-Carlton Golf Resort, Naples 172
South Walton County (Shark's Tooth)
27

Lawrence Packard
Westin Innisbrook Resort 96

Arnold Palmer
Arnold Palmer's Bay Hill Club &
Lodge 51
Palm Coast Resort 114

PGA National Resort & Spa 145
Saddlebrook Resort 91
Sawgrass Marriott Resort 42
World Golf Village 46

Jerry Pate
Bluewater Bay 15
Doral Golf Resort & Spa 140
Palm Beach Polo & Country Club 143
Sawgrass Marriott Resort (Valley
    Course) 42

Gary Player
Palm Coast 114

Donald Ross
Belleview Biltmore Resort & Spa 83
The Biltmore Hotel 125

Dick Wilson
Arnold Palmer's Bay Hill Club &
    Lodge 51
Doral Golf Resort & Spa 140

Index